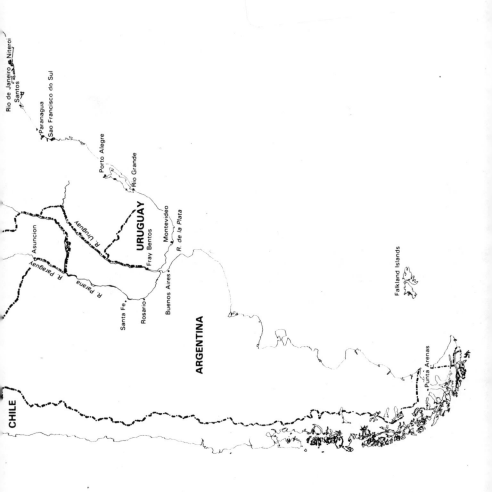

LAMPORT & HOLT

LAMPORT & HOLT

by

P. M. HEATON

THE STARLING PRESS LTD.
Printers & Publishers
RISCA   NEWPORT   GWENT
GREAT BRITAIN
1986

DEDICATION

To Lamports Old and Bold

ISBN 0 9507714 6 5

© First Edition December, 1986 : P. M. Heaton

Second Edition November, 1989

Published by P. M. Heaton, Pontypool, Gwent, NP4 OQF

Printed by Starling Press Ltd., Risca, Newport, Gwent, NP1 6YB

AUTHOR

Paul Michael Heaton was born at New Inn, Pontypool, in 1944 and was educated at Greenlawn Junior School in New Inn and the Wern Secondary School at Sebastopol. At fifteen he left school and commenced employment, at first in a local store and then with a builders' merchant. A year later he was appointed as a Deck Cadet in the Merchant Navy, with the Lamport and Holt Line of Liverpool, and served in their vessels *Chatham*, *Constable* and *Romney* usually in the Brazil and River Plate trades. He joined the Monmouthshire Constabulary (now Gwent) in 1963 and has served at Abergavenny, Cwmbran, Newport, the Traffic Department and as the Force Public Relations Officer, and now holds the rank of Inspector.

He has always maintained an interest in maritime history, and in the last ten years has had numerous articles published in the magazine *Sea Breezes*. He has had the following books published:

Reardon Smith 1905-1980.
The Redbrook: A Deep Sea Tramp.
The Usk Ships.
The Abbey Line.
Reardon Smith Line.
The South American Saint Line.
Welsh Blockade Runners in the Spanish Civil War.
The Baron Glanely of St. Fagans and W. J. Tatem Ltd.
    (with H. S. Appleyard).
Kaye, Son & Co. Ltd. (with K. O'Donoghue).

ACKNOWLEDGEMENTS

In compiling this history of the Lamport and Holt Line I would like to acknowledge my appreciation for the wealth of information and assistance freely given by the following:—

To Lamport and Holt Line Ltd., management and staff, current and past, both shorebased and seagoing—Messrs. D. A. Barber, E. V. Atkin, D. Green, R. W. Dutton, A. C. Berry, L. Ross, T. Waring, F. Evans, H. Binney, F. J. Page, M. Roberts and Captains T. Edgar, B. S. Haikney, B. M. Metcalf, D. C. Roberts, G. E. Roberts, H. W. Underhill, S. Dickinson, W. A. Sparks, J. I. Jones, W. A. Wilson and F. Martin.

To others for their assistance, including the World Ship Society Central Record Team, past and present—Messrs. G. H. Somner, H. S. Appleyard, K. O'Donoghue, P. L. White, A. L. Bland, L. Gray and the Rev. D. Ridley Chesterton; Messrs. W. A. Laxon of Auckland, New Zealand; E. K. Haviland of Baltimore, U.S.A.; G. Binns of Sao Paulo, Brazil; J. Lingwood, Sunderland; R. B. Bibby, Southampton; M. J. C. Bamford, Rocester; and to the Moss Hutchison Line Ltd., Liverpool, Austin & Pickersgill Ltd., Shipbuilders, Sunderland; and the National Maritime Museum, London.

To the following who have kindly provided photographs—Stewart Bale Ltd., Liverpool; A. Duncan, Gravesend; FotoFlite, Ashford; Harland and Wolff Ltd., Belfast; F. W. Hawks, Gillingham; J. A. Macleod, Liverpool; the Mariners Museum, Newport News; H. Matthews, Isle of Wight; the Peabody Museum, Salem; Tom Rayner, Ryde, Isle of Wight; Skyfotos Ltd., New Romney; Turners (Photography) Ltd., Newcastle on Tyne; the Walker Art Gallery, Liverpool; and the World Ship Photo Library.

A special thank you goes to Mr. C. J. M. Carter, the former Editor of the magazine *Sea Breezes* for all his help and encouragement throughout the years, and particularly with this project.

CONTENTS

LIST OF ILLUSTRATIONS

32. The "Vauban" of 1912 built for the New York, Brazil and River Plate trade. *(T. Rayner)*.
33. The "Vauban" of 1912. *(A. Duncan)*.
34. The liner "Vestris" of 1912 was lost in tragic circumstances in 1928. *(T. Rayner)*.
35. The "Archimedes" (2) joined the fleet in 1912. *(World Ship Photo Library)*.
36. Built in 1913 by A. McMillan and Son Ltd., Dumbarton, the "Pascal" (2) is seen on trials. *(T. Rayner)*.
37. The "Phidias" of 1913 served the Liverpool, Brazil and River Plate Steam Navigation Co. Ltd., for twenty-eight years, being a war loss in 1941. *(World Ship Photo Library)*.
38. The "Plutarch" of 1913. *(World Ship Photo Library)*.
39. The "Herschel" (3) of 1914 laid up in the River Dart in the early 1930s. *(World Ship Photo Library)*.
40. The refrigerated cargo liner "Meissonier" was built in 1915. *(World Ship Photo Library)*.
41. The "Meissonier" seen on charter to Union Castle. *(World Ship Photo Library)*.
42. The "Murillo" (1) was one of six refrigerated ships built in the First World War for the Liverpool, Brazil and River Plate Steam Navigation Co. Ltd. *(A. Duncan)*.
43. The "Moliere" of 1916. *(A. Duncan)*.
44. Built in 1917 the "Millais" (1) is seen on charter to Union Castle. *(A. Duncan)*.
45. The "Millais" (1). *(World Ship Photo Library)*.
46. The "Biela" (2) was one of twelve steamers acquired from the British Government after the First World War. *(A. Duncan)*.
47. The "Biela" was torpedoed and sunk in 1942 with the loss of all hands. *(World Ship Photo Library)*.
48. The "Bronte" (1) of 1919. *(World Ship Photo Library)*.
49. The "Browning" (1) of 1919. *(A. Duncan)*.
50. The "Balfe" of 1919. *(A. Duncan)*.
51. The "Bonheur" of 1920. *(A. Duncan)*.
52. The "Balzac" (1) of 1920 laid up in the River Dart in the depression of the early thirties. *(World Ship Photo Library)*.
53. The "Boswell" of 1920. *(A. Duncan)*.
54. The steamer "Laplace" (2) of 1919 was the first ship built to the company's own order following the First World War. *(A. Duncan)*.
55. The "Lalande" (2) of 1920. *(World Ship Photo Library)*.
56. Built in 1921 the "Linnell" was the first motorship to enter the fleet. *(A. Duncan)*.
57. The motorship "Leighton" of 1921. *(World Ship Photo Library)*.
58. The "Hogarth" (2) and "Browning" (1) laid up on the outside of a tier of ships in the Dart during the depression of the early 1930s. *(World Ship Photo Library)*.
59. The passenger liner "Vandyck" (3) was built in 1921 by Workman, Clark and Co. Ltd., Belfast. She is seen in her cruising livery shortly before the Second World War. *(Stewart Bale Ltd.)*.
60. The passenger liner "Voltaire" (2) of 1923. *(Stewart Bale Ltd.)*.
61. The "Voltaire" of 1923. *(World Ship Photo Library)*.
62. The "Delius" was the first of seven 'D' class cargo liners built for Lamport and Holt Line Ltd., by Harland and Wolff Ltd., Belfast between 1937 and 1945. The ship is seen on trials. *(Harland and Wolff Ltd.)*.
63. The "Delius" of 1937. *(A. Duncan)*.
64. The "Delane" of 1938. *(A. Duncan)*.
65. The "Devis" (1) of 1938 was a war loss in 1943. *(Harland and Wolff Ltd.)*.
66. A wartime view of the first "Devis" *(A. Duncan)*.
67. The "Defoe" (1) being launched at Harland and Wolff Ltd., Belfast in 1940. She was lost two years later. *(Harland and Wolff Ltd.)*.
68. The "Debrett" on trials in 1940. *(Harland and Wolff Ltd.)*.
69. The heavily armed "Debrett" during the Second World War. *(A. Duncan)*.

70. A post-war view of the "Debrett". *(Skyfotos Ltd.)*.
71. The "Devis" (2) of 1944. *(Skyfotos Ltd.)*.
72. The "Defoe" (2) of 1945. *(Skyfotos Ltd.)*.
73. The Polish liner "Batory" (14,287 gross tons) of 1936 was managed throughout the war by Lamport and Holt Line. *(Skyfotos Ltd.)*.
74. The Polish liner "Kosciuszko" of 1913 was managed by the company during the war. Following hostilities she was renamed "Empire Helford" by the Ministry of War Transport, the company continuing to manage her until the 1950s. *(T. Rayner)*.
75. The Troopship "Empire Bure" was managed by Lamport and Holt during the immediate post war period. *(T. Rayner)*.
76. The Troopship "Empire Test" managed by the company. *(T. Rayner)*.
77. The Troopship "Empire Test". *(T. Rayner)*.
78. Built in 1943 as the "Empire Bardolph", the "Memling" (3) was acquired in 1945. *(A. Duncan)*.
79. Formerly the "Empire Geraint" of 1942, the "Millais" (2) was purchased in 1945. *(World Ship Photo Library)*.
80. The "Dryden" (3) (ex "Empire Haig") served the company as such from 1946 to 1952. *(A. Duncan)*.
81. The "Dryden" (3) returned to Lamport and Holt in 1963 but under the name "Devis" (3). *(A. Duncan)*.
82. The Liberty ship "Lassell" (3) joined the fleet in 1947. *(Skyfotos Ltd.)*.
83. The "Lalande" (4) had previously been named "Byron" (2). *(A. Duncan)*.
84. The Victory ship "Vianna" was bareboat-chartered from Panama Shipping Company Inc. in 1947. *(T. Rayner)*.
85. Built in 1930 for the Booth Line, the "Bronte" (2) was transferred to Lamport and Holt in 1948. *(A. Duncan)*.
86. The "Spenser" (3) was acquired for the New York—Brazil and River Plate service in 1950. German built she had been taken as a war prize by the Royal Navy in 1939. *(A. Duncan)*.
87. Transferred from the New York Service to the United Kingdom in 1955 the "Spenser" was renamed "Roscoe". *(Skyfotos Ltd.)*.
88. The "Sallust" (2) was transferred from the Booth Line in 1951. *(World Ship Photo Library)*.
89. Built for the New York, Brazil and River Plate service in 1952, the "Siddons" (3) was a product of Wm. Pickersgill and Sons Ltd., Sunderland. *(World Ship Photo Library)*.
90. Transferred to the United Kingdom in 1955, the "Siddons" was renamed "Rubens" (2). *(A. Duncan)*.
91. Having spent two years with the Booth Line, the "Rubens" (ex "Siddons") returned to the Lamport and Holt Line in 1967 as the "Rossini". *(A. Duncan)*.
92. The turbine steamer "Romney" (2) was built in 1952 by Cammell Laird and Co. Ltd., Birkenhead. She was the company's flagship for over twenty years. *(Skyfotos Ltd.)*.
93. The "Romney" (2) had a career of twenty-six years under the Lamport and Holt Line houseflag. *(Skyfotos Ltd.)*.
94. The "Raeburn" (2) of 1952 was a product of Harland and Wolff Ltd., Belfast. *(Skyfotos Ltd.)*.
95. Having spent nineteen years with Blue Star Line or Austasia Line, the "Raeburn" (2) returned to Lamport and Holt in 1977 as the "Roland" (2). She was broken up in 1978. *(A. Duncan)*.
96. Built in 1939 as the "Columbia Star" for the Blue Star Line, the "Dryden" (4) was to spend two periods trading for Lamport and Holt between 1953 and 1968. *(Skyfotos Ltd.)*.
97. The "Raphael" (2) was built in 1953 by Bartram and Sons Ltd., Sunderland. *(Skyfotos Ltd.)*.
98. A rare view of the "Raphael" at Vancouver in 1959. *(F. W. Hawks)*.

99. The "Raphael" (2). (A. Duncan).
100. The small motorship "Verdi" (2) was acquired in 1955 for the direct Asuncion Service. (Capt. F. Martin).
101. The "Verdi" tied up to the river bank at Pto. Praia in the River Paraguay, just fifty miles from Asuncion. (Capt. F. Martin).
102. The small "Virgil" was bareboat-chartered from Panama Shipping Co. Inc., in 1956 for the Asuncion service. (A. Duncan).
103. The "Rossetti" (2) of 1956. (Skyfotos Ltd.).
104. The "Ronsard" of 1957 was a sistership of the "Raphael". (Skyfotos Ltd.).
105. The "Ronsard" was originally registered at Hamilton, Bermuda, transferring to the Liverpool Register in 1960. (A. Duncan).
106. The "Murillo" (3) was transferred from Blue Star in 1957. (A. Duncan).
107. The "Millais" (3) was another transfer from Blue Star in 1957. (A. Duncan).
108. The "Siddons" (4) was built in 1959 for the New York/West Indies/Amazon service. She is seen under her later name of "Veras" whilst on bareboat-charter to the Booth Steamship Co. Ltd. (A. Duncan).
109. The "Sheridan" (3) was built in 1961 for the New York/West Indies/Amazon service. (A. Duncan).
110. The refrigerated ship "Constable" was built in 1959 by Brooke Marine Ltd., Lowestoft. (Skyfotos Ltd.).
111. The "Chatham" (2) was a product of A. Stephen and Sons Ltd., on the Clyde. (Skyfotos Ltd.).
112. The motorship "Woodford" was chartered from Watts, Watts and Co. Ltd., in 1963, and renamed "Rossetti" (3). (A. Duncan).
113. The "Wanstead" was chartered in 1963 and renamed "Raeburn". (A. Duncan).
114. Having spent fifteen years with Booth Line and Austasia Line, the "Rubens" (3) was transferred to the Lamport and Holt Line in 1966. (Skyfotos Ltd.).
115. The "Rubens" (3) had been built in 1951. (A. Duncan).
116. The "Renoir" was acquired in 1967. She is seen with the Austasia Line funnel colours during a period on charter. (A. Duncan)
117. The steamship "Dunedin Star" built in 1950, was transferred in 1968 becoming the "Roland" (1). (A. Duncan).
118. Acquired in 1972, the "Raeburn" (4) was originally Blue Star Line's "Canadian Star". (A. Duncan).
119. Launched on October 31, 1978, the SD14 "Bronte" (3) is seen on Trials. (Turners (Photography) Ltd.).
120. The "Browning" (3) was one of four SD14 cargo ships built for the Lamport and Holt Line by Austin and Pickersgill Ltd., Sunderland. All were completed in the period 1979/80. (A. Duncan).
121. The "Browning" and her sisterships were equipped to carry 118-20ft containers. (Skyfotos Ltd.).
122. The SD14 cargo ship "Boswell" (3) of 1979. (Skyfotos Ltd.).
123. The launch of the "Belloc" at Austin and Pickersgill Ltd., Sunderland, on May 10, 1979. (Austin and Pickersgill Ltd.).
124. The SD14 "Belloc" of 1980. (Skyfotos Ltd.).
125. Built in 1979 as the "Ruddbank", the "Romney" (3) was acquired in 1983. (J. A. MacLeod).
126. Built in 1979 as the "New Zealand Star", the "Churchill" was lengthened at Singapore in 1986 for the Europe to East Coast of South America Container Service. (FotoFlite).
127. The "Churchill", with a capacity of 1,143 containers, is one of nine such ships operating in a Consortium between Europe and the East Coast of South America. (FotoFlite).
128. The "Churchill" entered Lamport and Holt Line service in April, 1986, when she commenced loading at Montevideo for Europe. She is seen in the English Channel in May, 1986, outward bound for Brazil. (FotoFlite).

1. INTRODUCTION

During one of my many visits to Newport Docks in my youth I saw an unusual motorship, the *Debrett,* which had part of her accommodation and the bridge incorporated into the funnel. I was impressed by her sheer workmanlike appearance and her recently painted and well maintained hull. Her funnel colours, blue with a black top divided by a white band were outstanding by their simplicity. Such was my interest that I established that she was owned by the Liverpool based shipping company, the Lamport and Holt Line, which operated services from the United Kingdom, Continent and New York to and from Brazil and the River Plate, and was in fact loading cargo for the latter region. In 1960 I was fortunate enough to be invited aboard this company's flagship, the turbine steamer *Romney* which was lying at Swansea, and again was impressed by the high standards to which the ship was maintained.

Further enquiries revealed that the Lamport and Holt Line was, like the Blue Star Line and the Booth Steamship Company, a part of the Vestey Group of companies. This was an organisation with which my grandfather had been employed before the Second World War at their meat processing plant, the Anglo Frigorifico at Dock Sud, Buenos Aires in the post of analytical chemist. Therefore, when in 1961, I decided to go to sea at the comparatively young age of sixteen years, it was little wonder that I should choose the Lamport and Holt Line, and be fortunate enough to be accepted as a Deck Cadet. At that time the company owned in excess of twenty ships and chartered in many more as and when required in order to maintain their services. In the following two and a half years I sailed in their vessels, *Chatham*, *Constable* and *Romney*, and worked-by on the *Rossetti* and *Dryden* at Liverpool.

Some decade or so later I started to take an interest in maritime history, and spent a number of years studying the history of this famous company. The Lamport and Holt Line had been established in 1845 when William James Lamport and George Holt had entered into partnership, and has had a continuous existence as shipowners to the present day. The result of my researches appeared in the shipping magazine *Sea Breezes* from June to December 1977, but since then a number of further developments have taken place, and as a result I decided to write this expanded volume devoted to the company's history.

I have started with an account of the founders' origins, followed by details of the various developments in the Lamport and Holt Line's history up to the present day when the container ship *Churchill* maintains their services. I hope that readers will be as fascinated by the company's history as much as I am, and to former L + H personnel I trust they will find that my efforts have been worthwhile.

P. M. Heaton.
December, 1986.

2. THE FOUNDERS—
WILLIAM JAMES LAMPORT
AND GEORGE HOLT

Established in 1845, the Lamport and Holt Line was the result of a partnership entered into by William James Lamport and George Holt.

Lamport, the senior partner, was born at Lancaster on the day of the Battle of Waterloo, June 18, 1815. His family origins can be traced back to France, thence via Devon to Lancashire, where his father was a Unitarian Minister. Subsequently in the 1830s he entered the offices at Liverpool of Messrs. Gibbs, Bright and Company, who were friends of his family. It was with this company that he acquired a practical knowledge of commerce and ship management which was later to earn him a place among Liverpool's leading shipowners. He assisted in the framing of the first Merchant Shipping Act and his extensive knowledge qualified him to be a sound adviser to the promoters of the Bill which was the result of Samuel Plimsoll's agitations for more tolerable conditions and for the greater safety of those who go to sea. His brother Charles was established as a shipbuilder at Workington, and a number of the partners' early sailing ships were built at this yard.

Much more is known of the other partner, George Holt. His family originated from Rochdale, a Lancashire textile town, from where his father George, senior, came in October 1807 to be apprenticed to a leading cotton broker Samuel Hope at premises in Water Street, Liverpool. In 1812 George senior was admitted as a partner in this business. In 1820 he married Emma Durning from whose family he rented a cottage in Rake Lane, Edge Hill. Three years later, by mutual agreement, George Holt senior and Samuel Hope separated their business interests. The latter entered banking whilst George remained in cotton, now trading as George Holt and Company.

George and Emma Holt had five sons; William who joined his father in the cotton business; George junior (born on September 19, 1824) who was to be co-founder of the Lamport and Holt Line; Alfred who served an apprenticeship to a railway engineer and later spent a short period with Lamport and Holt before founding his own shipping company, later to be known as the Blue Funnel Line; Robert Durning who became the first Lord Mayor of Liverpool in 1883; and Philip Henry who initially had a small interest in Lamport and Holt, but eventually left to become a partner with Alfred.

George junior was apprenticed in his youth to Thos. and Jno. Brocklebank, and it was whilst so serving that he met Lamport. He too was a worthy citizen, and associated himself with many beneficient institutions, becoming a supporter of Liverpool University, in connection with which he founded and endowed Chairs of Physiology and Pathology.

3. THE ENTRY INTO SHIPOWNING

Having decided to enter shipowning, Lamport who was now thirty years of age and the twenty-one year old Holt opened offices at Fenwick Buildings, Fenwick Street, Liverpool, but as the business grew they moved to larger premises in Drury Buildings, Water Street. Their first vessel, the barque *Christabel* of 335 tons was launched at Workington on September 17, 1845 and was financed by George Holt's father who initially held over half the shares in her, but on November 14 of the same year he transferred his 34 shares to the two partners and it was thus that they became shipowners. The vessel remained in their ownership for under a year, as she was sold to James Alexander of Workington on August 18, 1846.

George Holt senior was an extremely wealthy and influential gentleman, and he gave his wholehearted support to the venture, as indeed he did with all that his sons were involved in.

The partners' second ship was the barque *Junior* of 677 tons, built to their order at Quebec, and launched in the same year as the *Christabel*. Taken over on November 27, 1845 she sailed from Liverpool on December 23 under the command of Captain John Eills, who owned sixteen shares in her. This ship master was to hold shares in many of the partners' early ships, and was later to help Alfred Holt with the formation of his early fleet. The *Junior* was wrecked in 1855, the partners' first loss.

These early ships traded with the East Coast of North America, the River Plate, India, South Africa and the West Coast of South America, and many relatives, friends and associates of the partners were to hold shares in them, as was the custom in those days. Each ship was divided into 64 shares, and the profits for each voyage, after the subtraction of expenses and management fees by Lamport and Holt, were divided between shareholders.

As an example, the share position of Lamport and Holt's third ship is given in detail. She was the full rigged ship *William Ward*, of 755 tons, built at St. John, New Brunswick, in 1842, and bought by the partners on March 10, 1846. The shareholders were as follows.

Date	Shareholders/Transactions	No. of Shares
10.3.1846	William James Lamport and George Holt the younger, trading as Lamport and Holt.	56
	Robert Bibby and Jas. Fisher	8

Date	Shareholders/Transactions	No. of Shares
25.11.1846	Lamport and Holt transferred shares as follows:	
	to Thos. Fisher Moore	8
	to William Thornley	8
	to John Eills	4
19.6.1852	Thos. Fisher Moore transferred shares	
	to Lamport and Holt	8
15.1.1853	Lamport and Holt transferred shares	
	to Frederick McConnell	8
8.6.1853	The vessel was sold to William Morgan of Liverpool.	

One other vessel was acquired in 1846, this being the *Julius Caesar* of 738 tons, which remained in the fleet for six years.

Two full-rigged ships joined the fleet in 1847, the *Emma* built two years previously at Sunderland for George Holt senior, and the *Grasmere* of 454 tons built at Chepstow to the partners' own order. Of these the *Emma* was sold in 1852 to other Liverpool owners, whilst the latter ship spent almost eighteen years gainfully employed for Lamport and Holt. It is interesting to note that an original painting of the *Emma*, which had been named after George Holt's mother, which is housed in the Sudley Art Gallery and Museum at Liverpool, clearly shows the Lamport and Holt houseflag, which has remained unchanged to the present day.

The following year saw two further ships joining the fleet. The brig *Moslem* of 170 tons, acquired from J. Vale of London, remaining in the fleet for five years, while the full-rigger *Thornhill*, 698 tons, built to the order of the partners at Quebec, served them for just under eight years.

The fleet was now being rapidly expanded. Three further vessels were taken over in 1849; the 168 ton brig *Wilhelmina* acquired from James Moss and Company, the brigantine *Balkan*, 192 tons built at Liverpool to Lamport and Holt's order, and the barque *Napan Belle*, 332 tons, built in Nova Scotia.

In 1850, four more ships were added to the fleet, of which three were built to their own order. The full-rigger *Cathaya*, 407 tons built at the Workington yard of Lamport's brother Charles, which remained in the fleet until 1857 when she was lost; the schooner *Ceres*, 117 tons, built at Prince Edward Island, and the barque *Jane Morice*, 323 tons, built in New Brunswick. The fourth vessel, bought second hand, was the small brig

Margaret Gibson which Lamport and Holt had lengthened before putting her into service, thus increasing her tonnage from 124 to 148.

Whilst Lamport and Holt had been shipowners for five years, they were also in business as merchants, in that, as was fairly common in those days, they on occasions actually purchased the cargoes their ships carried, and whilst the vessel was on passage sold the cargo. This could be a very lucrative way of making a profit, as some of these cargoes were regarded as good investments, and were sometimes sold and resold many times during the passage of a vessel.

4. JAMES MOSS AND COMPANY— JOINT MEDITERRANEAN SERVICE

The next few years were to see great developments on the Mersey. Lamport and Holt had close connections with James Moss and Company, and were in fact trading in a joint service to the Mediterranean. James Moss and Company acquired their first three steamships for this service, and much of the specification for the vessels was undertaken by the Engineering Department of Lamport and Holt, who took shares in all three of them. The actual shareholdings are reproduced hereunder.

The steamer *Nile*, built of iron by Alexandra Denny and Brother of Dumbarton was of 347 tons.

Date	Shareholders/Transactions	No. of Shares
13.11.1850	Registered at Liverpool, owner being William Miles Moss, trading as James Moss and Company	64
16.11.1850	William Miles Moss transferred shares	
	to William James Lamport and George Holt the younger, trading as Lamport and Holt	8
1.4.1851	William Miles Moss transferred shares	
	to Lamport and Holt	16
2.7.1851	Lamport and Holt transferred shares	
	to George Holt, Cotton Broker	2
	to Charles Booth	2
	to Jas. Thornely	1
	to Wm. Schaw Lindsay	2
17.5.1851	Lamport and Holt transferred shares	
	to Thomas Fisher Moore	3
4.4.1853	Vessel sold and re-registered at Dublin.	

It is interesting to note the appearance of Lamport's cousin Charles Booth, the Corn Merchant, as two of his sons, Alfred and Charles, both served their time in the offices of Lamport and Holt, prior to establishing their own shipping company which was to trade to North Brazil and the River Amazon.

The *Orontes* built by the same builders as the *Nile*, but the following year, for James Moss and Company, had the following shareholders.

Shareholders	No. of Shares
Frederick Chapple	22
William Miles Moss	21
William James Lamport and George Holt the younger, trading as Lamport and Holt	7
George Holt, the elder, cotton broker	2
Charles Booth, senior	1
Wm. Rathbone and Samuel Martin, jointly	2
Wm. Rathbone, Wm. Rathbone, the younger, Samuel Greg Rathbone, and Thomas Kenyon Twist, jointly, trading as Rathbone Brothers	4
John Eills	2
Wm. Schaw Lindsay, London	2
Frederick McConnell	1

Alfred Holt, who at this time was employed in the Lamport and Holt offices, took a great interest in this ship and sailed in her late in 1851 on her maiden voyage to Egypt. On his return he spent some time on the design of the next Moss steamer, the *Scamander* of 753 tons, built in 1854 by Stothert and Company, Clifton, Gloucestershire, another iron steamer. The shareholders in the *Scamander* were as follows.

Shareholders	No. of Shares
Wm. Miles Moss and Frederick Chapple, jointly	52
William James Lamport and George Holt the younger trading as Lamport and Holt	4

Shareholders	No. of Shares
Wm. Rathbone,	4
Wm. Rathbone the younger,	
Samuel Greg Rathbone, and	
Thomas Kenyon Twist,	
trading as Rathbone Brothers	
Wm. Schaw Lindsay	4

Clearly most of the above people held shares in each other's ships, and thus also had an interest in Lamport and Holt's early venture into shipowning.

In 1852 the small barque *Rydel* of 262 tons joined the Lamport and Holt fleet having been built to their own order in New Brunswick. She was to remain in their ownership only a matter of months before passing to Rathbone Brothers. Between 1853 and 1854 two small ships were purchased second hand. They were the *Princeza*, a brig of 149 tons built in 1849, and the schooner *Queen*, a vessel of 104 tons built in 1848 at Teignmouth; remaining in the fleet for eight and five years respectively, before being sold for further trading.

So it was that in something less than ten years, the two partners had acquired a fleet of thirteen sailing ships trading worldwide, and had substantial shares in a number of other vessels, including the rapidly expanding fleet of steamers of James Moss and Company, trading mainly to Egypt.

It was in 1854, at the outbreak of the Crimean War, that a number of these ships were employed in the transport of stores and equipment for the British and French Governments, as were those of James Moss and Company.

The *Breeze*, a small snow of 165 tons, joined the fleet in 1855, having previously been owned by J. Nicholson of Annan, for whom she was built at that port in 1848. She was to remain in Lamport and Holt's service for some thirteen years. The other acquisition was the ship *Simoda* of 697 tons, built at St. John, New Brunswick; she was wrecked after only about a year's service.

Three more vessels were delivered to the partners' order in 1856. The *Memphis* was a wooden barque of 416 tons built at St. John, New Brunswick, while the barque *Kahlamba* of 319 tons built at Port Glasgow, was the only iron sailing ship ever to be owned by the partners. Of these the former traded for six years before disposal to Phillips and Company of Liverpool for further trading, while the *Kahlamba* served the partners for some thirteen years before disappearing from Lloyds' Register.

However, the *Agenoria*, a full-rigged ship of 1,023 tons built at New Brunswick, and at that time the largest ship owned by Lamport and Holt, served for twelve years before her sale to Griffiths and Company, Liverpool. Subsequently she passed to S. Young of North Shields and was broken up there in 1885.

Four barques and a ketch were acquired in 1857, three of which were delivered from the Workington shipyard of Lamport's brother Charles. They were the barques *Blencathra*, *Coniston* and *Glaramara* of 466, 204 and 475 tons respectively. The *Elizabeth Morrow* was the other barque, delivered from New Brunswick, a vessel of 394 tons. The 156 ton ketch *Old Harry*, fourteen years old, was the fifth purchase during this year.

This year marked the introduction into the fleet of the first steamer to be owned and managed by the partners, the small *Zulu* of 189 tons, built at Greenock. She was to trade to South Africa and later to the West Indies, remaining in the fleet until August 7, 1858, when sold to owners at Port Louis, Mauritius. She was wrecked on Folly Point, Jamaica on May 28, 1861.

The *Zulu* was to be the only steamer in the Lamport and Holt fleet during this period, Mr. Lamport, the senior partner, remaining unconvinced, even with their interest in the Moss steamers, that this new form of propulsion was going to last—a view held by many influential shipowners of the time. Their answer was to continue buying and operating sailing ships, while building an increasing shareholding in the steamships of the period, thereby assuring the future by having interests in both.

A further Workington-built vessel, the 198 ton schooner *Rothay* was launched to the partners' order in 1858, but she was to remain in their possession for only six years. The barque *Thebes* was purchased from Rathbone Brothers, having traded for them since her completion in 1850 at Sunderland. A vessel of 432 tons, she remained in the Lamport and Holt fleet for four years before passing to E. S. Roberts of London in 1862. In 1859 a 526 ton barque, the *Eddystone* was built in New Brunswick for the partners, but after only a year was sold to Young of North Shields.

5. THE LIVERPOOL, BRAZIL AND RIVER PLATE STEAM NAVIGATION CO. LTD.

In 1861 the partners bowed to the inevitable, and ordered two brig-rigged iron steamers. The *Memnon* (1,290 gross tons) was delivered in 1861 by Scott and Company, Greenock, and the *Copernicus* (1,372 gross tons) was completed the following year by A. Leslie and Company, Hebburn-on-Tyne. This shipyard was to deliver a considerable number of vessels to the partners over the next three decades. These ships were usually employed in the joint service with James Moss and Company to the Mediterranean where their increased capacity was found to be most useful.

It was with these early steamers that the practise of naming the ships after prominent persons connected with the arts and sciences was adopted. The *Memnon* was sold in 1883 to Alfred Holt's Ocean Steamship Company for whom she traded in Far Eastern Waters until hulked in 1899. The *Copernicus* passed to French owners in 1864 and continued trading until broken up in January, 1890.

With the delivery of these ships the partners did not abandon their interest in sailing ships, but continued to acquire secondhand tonnage and order new vessels of increased size. So it was, in the same year that the *Memnon* was delivered that a full-rigged ship of 1,027 tons was delivered by McLachlan of New Brunswick, named *Bonnie Dundee*. She served Lamport and Holt until sold for further trading on December 31, 1872. In 1862 two more sailing ships arrived; the new barque *Chalgrove* (509 tons) was built to their order by Charles Lamport at Workington, remaining in the partners' ownership until 1869, although she was afloat under various other owners until broken up in 1896. The second vessel was the full-rigged ship *Nazarine* of 921 tons, built in 1854 at Quebec for Fisher and Sons, from whom the partners acquired her. She served them for the next three years before her sale to other Liverpool owners.

For some considerable time both Alfred Holt, who was now fairly well established on his own account, and Philip Henry Holt, who held a small interest in Lamport and Holt, had been urging Lamport, the senior partner, to start a really good steamship line in one of the Atlantic trades. Lamport took a good deal of persuasion, for although his attitude to steamers had changed, he still did not believe in lines of steamers. But eventually he yielded and ordered a new vessel from A. Leslie and Company for the Brazil and River Plate trade. She was an iron, brig-rigged steamer of 1,500 gross tons, completed in 1863 and named *Kepler*. Having taken a great interest in her construction, Alfred Holt sailed in her on her maiden voyage to Brazil and the River Plate via Lisbon.

Clement Jones in his book *Pioneer Shipowners* refers to this new venture.

> From a small beginning that huge Brazil and River Plate undertaking was started against the wish (or with the complete indifference) of Lamport and Holt, and owing to the persistence of Alfred and Philip Henry Holt. A study of the history of shipping shows us that some are born to a trade, others acquire trades, while some like Mr. Lamport have trades thrust upon them.

However, Lamport and Holt did not invest all in the new venture, for in the same year as the *Kepler* appeared in the fleet a new brigantine, a second *Christabel* was delivered by Owen of Teignmouth to the partners. A small vessel of 170 tons, she was sold the following year, and having passed through numerous owners eventually became a hulk at Plymouth in 1903.

January, 1864 saw the termination of Philip Henry Holt's connection with the partners, and he joined his brother Alfred in the management of his company from India Buildings, Liverpool. Thereafter they made the plans and laid the foundations for their important service to the Far East. However, it is interesting to note that when there was a temporary slump in their trade, as occurred from time to time, that one or more of their ships was placed on the Lamport and Holt berth for a voyage or voyages to the East Coast of South America.

During 1864 two new steamers joined the fleet, and were placed into the new South American liner service. They were the *Newton* of 1,329 gross tons built by McNab and Company, and the *Galileo* of similar tonnage delivered by A. Leslie and Company on the Tyne. Of these first three steamers built specifically for the Brazil and River Plate trade, the *Kepler* remained in the fleet for forty years until broken up in 1903, having been lengthened in 1871 and had new engines and boiler fitted. The *Newton* lasted until April 9, 1881 when she was wrecked off Madeira, while on passage Rio de Janeiro to London. The *Galileo* was sold in 1872, and after a number of changes of ownership was lost in 1898.

But the partners kept alive their interest in sailing ships, and they still held their interest in the Moss ships. In 1865 a further two new sailing ships joined the fleet; the *Sumroo* a barque of 612 tons built by Hilyard of New Brunswick, and the full-rigged ship *Timour* of 1,331 tons from the same yard. This last vessel was the largest sailing ship owned by the partners up to that date. The *Sumroo* remained in Lamport's ownership for only a few months and likewise the *Timour* was sold later that year, to Rathbone Brothers. This same year saw the arrival of five steamers in the fleet.

25

Two ships that had previously been in Alfred Holt's fleet trading to the West Indies were acquired. The *Saladin* built in 1856, and the *Talisman* of 1860 had both been sold to the West India and Pacific Steamship Company in 1864, from whom they were bought by the partners in the following year. However, not all the shares in the *Talisman* were acquired until 1869. The former remained in the fleet until sold in 1872 and the latter foundered on January 21, 1873, North West of Burlings, Portugal. The *Herschel* built in 1853 on the Mersey by Laird as the *Cubana* was bought the same year, and remained under their house flag for some seven years. The other two acquisitions during this year were the *Ptolemy* and *Halley* delivered by the Hebburn yard of A. Leslie and Company. The latter served her owners until 1895 when broken up, being outlasted by the *Ptolemy* by a year.

The enterprise had developed so well, and the size of the fleet was growing so rapidly that the partners decided to form a limited company under the title of The Liverpool, Brazil and River Plate Steam Navigation Company Limited, of which the partnership became managers. This transaction took effect from December 18, 1865. Previously the ships had been operated on the 64 share system, whereby the voyage profits less management fees and expenses of each vessel were divided amongst shareholders in specific vessels. Under the new system the shareholders were allocated shares in the new company, and received dividends from the profits of the company as a whole. This was a far less risky proposition, as under the old system shareholders could be liable for unlimited losses, whereas with a limited company they were only liable for their actual shareholding.

The year 1866 was one of great development in the fleet, two further sailing ships being acquired, but the staggering number of seven steamers were acquired, six of them being delivered from the yard of A. Leslie and Company. In addition a small collier, about one year old, the *Ironsides* was purchased. The full-rigger *March* of 1,255 tons was delivered from Hilyard, New Brunswick, and was to remain in the fleet for less than a year. The second sailing ship was the *Manchester*, a brigantine of 158 tons, built as far back as 1824 at Whitehaven for T. and J. Brocklebank, the firm in which George Holt had served his apprenticeship. She was sold by them in 1852 to Armstrong of Whitehaven, before arriving in the Lamport and Holt fleet in 1866, for whom she traded until 1873 when broken up. The six Leslie built, brig-rigged iron steamers were the *Cassini* (sold 1872), *Copernicus* (2) (wrecked in February, 1883), *Donati* (sold 1891), *Flamsteed* (1) (lost in collision on November 24, 1873), *Laplace* (1) and *Humboldt* (both sold in 1894). The seventh ocean going vessel was the *La Plata* bought from other owners, but she too was a product of A. Leslie and Company.

The collier *Ironsides* is of interest, as a short account of her early master appears in the forword of a navigation book entitled *Wrinkles in Practical Navigation* by Captain S. T. C. Lecky, Master Mariner, Commander R.N.R., F.R.A.S., F.R.G.S., Extra Master; Younger Brother, Trinity House; from which the following passage is quoted.

During 1865 this company was wound up, and at the end of August his connection with the *Krishna* perforce came to an end. 'But' wrote the indomitable Lecky, 'my luck still held good, for I immediately got command of a screw collier, trading between Liverpool, Cardiff and elsewhere.'

This vessel was the *Ironsides* of 514 tons, belonging to Mr. Robert Girvan, of Liverpool. What luck indeed. There are few sailors who would consider themselves fortunate in having given up the Inman Line (a reference to the company with which he served before his service in the *Krishna*) to find themselves on board a collier.

He admitted however in later years that, luck or no luck, although it had not been pleasant work, it had given him fresh opportunities and new experience in a strange trade. It was his first real command, and he was undoubtably fortunate in getting even such a humble one within so short a time of obtaining his master's certificate (September 13, 1864; extra master's certificate October 27, 1864. He was also qualified in the Board of Trade examination in steam machinery). The experience added greatly to his general usefulness and to the store of knowledge of all classes of ships which he was accumulating.

On February 17, 1866, the screw collier master, now in his 28th year, was gazetted a sub-lieutenant in the Royal Naval Reserve, and for various periods in 1867 and early 1868, while his ship was discharging, he was devoting his short holidays to putting in his drills on board H.M.S. *Eagle* at Liverpool; and having satisfactorily qualified he was gazetted as a Lieutenant R.N.R. to date January 14, 1868.

'Those were the days', he wrote, 'in which there were no retaining fees for R.N.R. officers, nor was there any allowance for uniform and equipment, so I spent far more on the R.N.R. than ever returned to me'.

It will be within the experience of many that, if treated loyally, a humble appointment very often becomes the stepping stone to something a good deal better, and it was a source of considerable gratification to Lecky to find suddenly that his inconspicuous collier had been purchased by Messrs. Lamport and Holt, the well known shipowners of Liverpool, who were trading as the Liverpool, Brazil and River Plate Steam Navigation Co. Ltd., and who retained him as master and kept on all his officers. He remained in the *Ironsides* for another eight months with his new owners and left her on August 17, 1867.

Thenceforward his career ran pleasantly enough in the well-equipped, comfortable steamers of this great company trading between Liverpool and the principal ports of Eastern South America. He commanded successively over a period of four years their steamships:- *Ironsides*; *Cassini*, 687 tons—three months; the chartered ship *Uruguay*, 856 tons—thirteen months; and the *Halley*, 995 tons—sixteen months, and became well known in connection with them.

He resigned his position in the *Halley* at Liverpool on October 21, 1870, following a dispute with George Holt, in which, from the text of this forward, it would appear that Mr. Lamport disagreed with his partner. Whatever, Lamport sent Lecky £100 from his own pocket, but Lecky would not return to the company.

The *Ironsides* remained in the fleet until 1868 when she was sold to D. Jones of Briton Ferry.

In 1866 the company's ramifications were greatly enlarged with services from London, Glasgow and Antwerp to the East Coast of South America. It is interesting to note that a service also commenced in later years serving the West Coast of this great continent. The *Halley* inaugurated the first direct service between Antwerp and the River Plate in that same year. Eventually a contract was obtained from the Belgian Government for the carriage of mails.

A third *Christabel* was acquired in 1867, built by King of New Brunswick, a barque of 660 tons, she traded under their colours for two years. A second sailing ship, the full-rigged *Tidal Wave* of 1,280 tons, was launched for them at New Brunswick, but was quickly disposed of. Two steamers were delivered to the partners from the yard of A. Leslie and Company in 1867, the *Tycho Brahe* and *Hipparchus*, both of about 1,800 gross tons. The former ship remained under Lamport and Holt's colours until sold in 1882 to a Mr. Charles Wells, better known as the man who broke the bank at Monte Carlo. He appropriately renamed her as the *Palais Royale*, but sold her to Turkish owners in 1884. On October 30, 1908 whilst named *Taif*, she was lost in a collision. The *Hipparchus* was converted to a hulk in 1895 and served as such for a further twenty years.

In 1869 the *Halley* became the first iron steamer to transport a coffee shipment from Rio de Janeiro to New York, thus breaking with the old idea that it would spoil the flavour to carry coffee in anything other than a wooden sailing ship. This was a turning point in the company's affairs, in that they now started trading direct from the River Plate and Brazil to United States East Coast ports, and on occasions returned back to South

America, or to the United Kingdom with the raw materials for the cotton industry.

The same year saw the last sailing ship enter the fleet, the full-rigged ship *Sarah J. Eills* of 1,350 tons, named after the wife of Captain John Eills who, as previously seen, held command and an interest in some of the early ships. She was built by King of St. John, but only remained in their ownership for about two years.

Another Hebburn-built iron steamer arrived in 1869, the *Pascal* of about 2,000 gross tons. She was eventually broken up in 1897.

Due to the rapid growth of the steamer services to South America from the United Kingdom, Antwerp and the United States, the company went through a period of consolidation, in that steamers, of ever increasing size (although today little larger than short-sea traders), continued to join the fleet. Most continued to come from the Hebburn yard of A. Leslie and Company, while the sailing ships were rapidly disposed of. Although, as previously mentioned, the *Sarah J. Eills* joined the fleet during 1869, no less than six other sailing ships were disposed of.

Three more steamers were commissioned in 1870, two being Hebburn-built, and just over 2,000 gross tons, the *Olbers* and *Biela*. Both were to serve the company for some thirty years, the *Olbers* being broken up in Italy in 1901, while the *Biela* was lost in a collision on October 1, 1900 with the steamer *Eagle Point* off Nantucket, while on passage from New York to Liverpool. The third acquisition in that year was the first vessel to bear the name *Vandyck* in the fleet. Bought from another famous Liverpool company—T. and J. Harrison, for whom she had traded as the *Warrior*, she had originally been launched in 1867 as the *City of Limerick* for Tait and Company of London by Randolph Elder and Company, Fairfield. The *Vandyck* traded for Lamport and Holt until 1892 when she was converted to a hulk at Rio de Janeiro.

The *Calderon* and *Camoens* of 1,018 and 1,093 gross tons respectively, arrived in 1871, the former remaining until sold to Brazil in 1887. The latter was sold some six years earlier to a Leith firm, and continued afloat, later under the Italian flag until broken up in 1923 after a creditable career of some fifty-two years, a fine testimonial to her original builders—A. Leslie and Company.

Three new ships followed in 1872 and were of interest in that they all appeared from different yards. The *Gassendi* of 1,849 gross tons, from Hall, Russell and Company, Aberdeen, (sold 1885), the *Rubens* of 1,671 gross tons from Iliff, Moundey and Company, Sunderland, which was in her later years to spend so much time at Punta Arenas as a store ship before being sold at that port as a hulk in 1909, and the *Lalande* of 1,048 gross tons, built by A. and J. Inglis and Company, Glasgow (sold 1885).

29

Seven ships hoisted the Lamport and Holt flag in 1873 for the first time, two of which were purchased from other owners. The *Teniers* of 1868 from Tait and Company, for whom she had traded as the *City of Rio de Janeiro*, and the *Memling* launched the previous year by Gourlay and Company, Dundee, as the *Malaga* for Malcolm and Company. Four yards were responsible for the delivery of the other five ships that year. A. Leslie and Company for the *Galileo* and *Leibnitz* of some 2,000 gross tons each. The *Galileo* was the second ship in the fleet to bear the name, the previous one having been sold in 1870. Both were to have long careers with the company. The *Maraldi* of 1,002 gross tons from the Whitehaven Shipbuilding Company was to remain in the fleet for only two years as she was wrecked on February 28, 1875 near Pernambuco, while on passage Montevideo to Antwerp. The *Delambre* and *Thales* came from William Hamilton and Co. Ltd., Port Glasgow, and Hall, Russell and Company, Aberdeen, respectively. Both flew the Lamport and Holt houseflag for many years.

The end of an era was marked in 1874 when William James Lamport died at New Brighton. He had achieved outstanding success during his lifetime as a merchant shipowner and had been highly regarded by all connected with the industry. He was succeeded in the partnership by Walter Holland, who had been a fellow apprentice with George Holt in the firm of Thos. and Jno. Brocklebank, and Charles W. Jones who had served his apprenticeship with Lamport and Holt.

Four new steamers arrived during 1874. These were the *Archimedes* (sold 1893), *Cervantes* (sold 1884), *Maskelyne* (foundered on January 31, 1903 in position 41.35′N, 34.40′W, while on passage New Orleans to Antwerp) and finally the *Hevelius* (broken up in 1903). The following year the *Rosse* arrived (sold to Brazil in 1898).

The *Canova* of 1,120 gross tons joined the fleet in 1876, yet another product from the yard of A. Leslie and Company, Hebburn-on-Tyne. She was followed a year later by the *Euclid*, *Horrox* and *Plato* from Hall, Russell and Company, Aberdeen, T.R. Oswald, Southampton and A. Leslie and Company, respectively. Of these the *Canova* was to remain in the fleet for only seven years, the *Horrox* served the company until broken up in 1903, and the *Euclid* passed to Brazilian owners in 1898 and was broken up six years later. The *Plato* was lost after fifteen years service, when she foundered 160 miles off the Scilly Isles on March 1, 1892, having broken her main shaft the previous day while on a voyage from Liverpool to Brazil.

Some idea of the importance of Lamport and Holt can be seen in the following advertisement which appeared in the first issue of the English language newspaper, the Buenos Aires Herald in September, 1876. As can be seen passengers, both saloon and steerage, were carried in all vessels, and a surgeon served on all the ships. Lamport and Holt was by far the largest carrier from South America to and from the United Kingdom, Belgium and the United States.

STEAM TO NEW YORK

Lamport and Holt's Line of Steamers
Under contract with the Brazilian Government
The splendid steamship
Tycho Brahe
1,848 tons
Miller, Commander
Will leave this Port on the 18th
September for

NEW YORK

via Rio de Janeiro, Bahia and Pernambuco and Para
(leaving Rio de Janeiro on 1st October)

Rates of Passage Money

	1st class	3rd class
New York	$.197.20	$.85.40
Para	130	49
Pernambuco	90	40
Bahia	70	35
Rio de Janeiro	50	25

All the steamers of this Line are repleted with every comfort, and carry a Surgeon and a Stewardess.

Liverpool, Brazil and River Plate Steamers
Lamport and Holt's Line
Departures
S.S. *Kepler,* for Havre and Liverpool
Will leave on 15th September.

S.S. *Tycho Brahe*, for New York
Will leave on the 18th September
and Rio de Janeiro 1st October.

S.S. *Hipparchus*, for Antwerp and Liverpool
Will leave this port on 25th September
(carrying the Belgian Mails.)

S.S. *Delambre*, for Antwerp and Liverpool
Will leave this port on 30th September
Receiving Cargo in the River Parana.

S.S. *Hevelius*, for Antwerp and Liverpool
Will leave on Monday, 9th October
(carrying the Belgian Mails.)

Rates of Passage Money		
	1st	*3rd*
Southampton, Liverpool, Havre and Antwerp	£35	£15
Lisbon	30	12
Bahia	12	7
Rio de Janeiro	10	5
New York	40	17.10

In the Mail Steamers Table Wine is supplied gratis to all passengers.
First Class Return Tickets are issued (with a reduction of 25%),
available for 12 months.
All the steamers of this Line carry Surgeons and Stewardesses, and
are replete with every comfort.

Pre-Paid Passages

Are issued to parties wishing to bring out their friends from England,
at the following rates:—

1st	£32
3rd Class	£14

Apply to Agents:—

Henry A. Green and Co.

Or to the Brokers:—

Green, LeRosignol and Co.
80, Reconquista.

Agents in Rosario:—

John Thompson and Co.

---

6. SOCIETE DE. NAV. ROYALE BELGE SUD-AMERICAINE AND THE ARGENTINE STEAM LIGHTER CO. LTD.

The volume of cargo carried to and from Antwerp had steadily built up since that first sailing from the Belgian port by the *Halley* some eleven years earlier, so much so that, with their important contract to carry mails for the Belgian Government, it was thought necessary to transfer a number of ships to the Belgian flag. So it was that in 1877 a new company, Societe de. Nav. Royale Belge Sud-Americaine was formed, with offices at Quai Jordaens No. 1, Antwerp. The formation was marked with the transfer of the *Copernicus* (2) from the British to the Belgian flag in that year, followed in 1878 by no less than seven ships, the *Kepler*, *Tycho Brahe*, *Hipparchus*, *Pascal* (1), *Teniers*, *Rosse* and *Horrox*. These eight ships were to carry on this important trade supplemented as required by units of the parent company.

The *Pliny*, *Bessel* and *Sirius* joined the Lamport and Holt fleet in 1878, the former coming from the yard of the Barrow Construction Co. Ltd., while the *Bessel* was yet another product from A. Leslie and Company. Both were to be lost while in the company's service. The *Pliny* was wrecked off Long Branch, New Jersey, while on passage Rio de Janeiro to New York with a cargo of coffee on May 13, 1882, while the *Bessel* was lost in collision with the Wilson Line's *Hero* in the English Channel on June 22, 1895, on passage London to Brazil. The *Sirius* came from Rathbone Brothers for whom she had been built in 1869, and remained in the fleet until broken up in 1899.

Two further iron steamers built at Hebburn arrived in 1879; the second *Herschel* (schooner-rigged) and the *Lassell* (brig-rigged), both of about 1,950 gross tons. The *Herschel* was badly damaged on November 17, 1901 in the Crosby Channel, River Mersey, in a collision with the steamer *Ardeola*. Damage was so severe that she was not thought worthy of repair and was sold to Dutch shipbreakers early the following year. The *Lassell* continued in the fleet until sold to New York owners in 1900, and some twenty years later appeared under the Moroccan flag, eventually being broken up in 1924.

A steam tug, the *Stella* (106 gross tons) was acquired in 1880, being built by the Liverpool Forge Company, she was destined for service in the River Plate. She was sold on July 6, 1894 for further trading. Also in 1880 the *Nasmyth* appeared from Leslie's yard, followed a year later by the *Mozart*, *Handel* and *Dalton* from the same yard, the *Strabo* from the Barrow Construction Co. Ltd., and the *Cavour* from Scott and Company, Greenock. Of these the *Nasmyth* and *Mozart* were broken up in 1902, followed by the *Strabo* three years later, but the *Handel* went to an Italian firm in 1902 for nine years further trading. The *Dalton* was wrecked on September 28, 1895 on the Isle of Islay, on passage New York to the Clyde.

The *Cavour* was an interesting vessel of 618 gross tons, as she was one of three shallow draft vessels which operated a coastal passenger service on behalf of the Brazilian Government, the other two ships coming from the same yard two years later as the *Chatham* and *Canning*. When in 1891 it was decided by the Brazilians to run their own service all three were sold to them, becoming the *Itapeva*, *Itauna* and *Itatiaya* respectively. All three were subsequently broken up at Rio de Janeiro in the early 1930s, having been afloat for about fifty years.

In 1882 came the *Holbein*, *Hogarth* and *Flaxman*, all of just over 2,000 gross tons. The *Holbein* was sold in 1901 to Manchester owners and thence to Spain for whom she traded until broken up in 1930. The *Hogarth* and *Flaxman* were disposed of in 1902 and 1903 respectively, the former being broken up in 1922. However the *Flaxman* traded until she sank on August 24, 1932 while on passage Rio de Janeiro to Manous.

Apart from the *Chatham* and *Canning* previously mentioned, two other steamers arrived in 1883 from Hebburn; the *Cuvier* of 2,299 gross tons and *Buffon* of 2,304 gross tons. The former was lost in collision with the Norwegian steamer *Dovre* off the East Goodwin Lightship, on March 3, 1900, while on a voyage from Antwerp to Brazil whilst under the command of Captain William Spratly. There were only three survivors, the lookout, the man at the wheel and the Second Officer. The *Buffon* went to Brazil in 1908 and became a First World War casualty on May 20, 1917 when torpedoed and sunk by a submarine off Ushant.

An interesting development took place in 1884 when Lamport and Holt formed a new subsidiary under the title of the Argentine Steam Lighter Co. Ltd., for the purpose of operating passenger and cargo services in and around the River Plate. The new company operated until about 1900, and during this period had the following vessels which were all registered at Liverpool, and either used Montevideo or Buenos Aires as their survey port.

Name	Year Built	Gross Tons
Amadeo	1884	411
Brenda	1884	411
Como	1885	477
Delta	1886	289
Elena	1886	289

Name	Year Built	Gross Tons
Freda	1888	498
Gerda	1888	498
Hilda	1889	537
Ida	1889	561
Juanita	1895	719
*Luna	1889	193

* This vessel was actually registered in the ownership of the parent company—the Liverpool, Brazil and River Plate Steam Navigation Co. Ltd.

Of these ships, the *Luna* survived in the River Plate under different owners until well into the mid 1960s. The pioneer ship *Amadeo* was sold in 1892 and was eventually beached in the 1930s in the Straits of Magellan at San Gregorio, where she survives to the present day.

The year 1885 saw the arrival of the two year old *Caxton* and three new ships, the *Garrick*, *Spenser* and *Dryden* of about 2,500 gross tons each. The *Garrick* was sold in 1906 to a Norwegian company for whom she became a whaling ship, but was wrecked on November 10 of that year on South Georgia Island whilst on her first voyage for them. The *Spenser* and *Dryden* passed to T. Hogan and Sons in 1895 becoming the *Manitou* and *Menemsha*; the former passed to Italian owners in 1899 and was finally broken up in 1909, while the latter ship went to the United States Navy as a transport in 1898, being resold to commercial owners in 1921, and was finally broken up in 1928 at San Francisco.

The *Chaucer* appeared from the Hebburn yard of R. and W. Hawthorn, Leslie and Co. Ltd., in 1886, this being the new style of A. Leslie and Company. She was of 2,769 gross tons, and was disposed of in 1913 for demolition. Also acquired during this year was the *Siddons* delivered by Oswald, Mordaunt of Southampton, and of 2,846 gross tons. She was sold in 1894 to Ballingall and Garroway of Glasgow and lost on April 18, 1896 in collision with the steamer *Graigearb* off Norderney, while on passage Odessa to Hamburg.

In the same year the *Olbers* and *Galileo* were transferred to the Belgian flag to supplement the seven of the original eight ships transferred to that flag.

Two years passed before the next vessels were acquired, in 1888. The third *Copernicus*, having been built the previous year by Oswald, Mordaunt and Company, Southampton, as the *Lilian* for E. Bates and Sons, Liverpool, was at that time, at 3,230 gross tons, the largest ship in the Lamport and Holt fleet. The other two acquisitions were the *Newton* (second of that name to serve in the fleet) of 2,540 gross tons, from R. and W. Hawthorn, Leslie and Co. Ltd., and the *Milton* of 2,679 gross tons from the Glasgow yard of D. and W. Henderson and Co. Ltd. The *Copernicus* was lost on October 16, 1895 when she was posted missing on passage from Sandy Point to Valparaiso. The *Newton* was broken up at Antwerp in 1910, and the following year on June 15, the *Milton* was wrecked off Portugal, near Cabo Espichel, on passage London to Santos.

The year 1889 saw two ships join the fleet from the Star Navigation Co. Ltd. (Rathbone Bros), Liverpool. They were the *Wordsworth* (3,260 gross tons) of 1882, previously the *Capella*, and the *Coleridge* of 1875 (2,561 gross tons) previously the *Mira*. Both were products of A. Leslie and Company, Hebburn-on-Tyne. The *Wordsworth* remained in the fleet until wrecked near Bahia on passage from New York on August 1, 1902. The *Coleridge* was broken up at Marseilles in June, 1904.

This year saw three ships transferred to the Belgian flag, the *Leibnitz*, *Maskelyne* and *Hevelius*, followed a year later by the *Wordsworth* and *Coleridge*.

Two Hawthorn, Leslie built ships arrived in 1890, the *Chantrey* and *Phidias*. The latter lasted until 1911 when she was sold to Brazil and, renamed *Tupy*, was wrecked near Agadir on September 21, 1918. The *Chantrey* was wrecked on October 17, 1896 near Valparaiso while on passage from Guayaquil. Only one ship joined the fleet in the following four years, that being the *Flamsteed* in 1892 from Hebburn. Like the two previously mentioned ships, she too was wrecked, being lost on March 26, 1893 on the coast of Chile, near Imperial River, on a voyage from Antwerp to Valparaiso, the wreck being sold locally for scrap.

While the company had over three decades followed the principal of naming ships after poets, artists, etc., hitherto they had not had a series of names for ships of a particular size, type or trade, except on isolated occasions. From 1895 it became the rule rather than the exception to name similar ships in classes beginning with the same letter. Thus in 1895 two 'H' class and three 'C' class ships joined the fleet. The *Homer* and *Cavour* came from the yard of Sir Raylton Dixon and Co. Ltd., Middlesbrough, while D. and W. Henderson and Co. Ltd., Glasgow delivered the *Horace*, *Canova* and *Cervantes*. The 'H' class were of 2,585 and 3,335 gross tons respectively, while the 'C' class were of between 4,600 and 5,000 gross tons. In fact the *Cavour* of 4,978 gross tons was the largest ship in the fleet up to that date. Of these the *Homer* was sold in 1912, becoming the *Odila* under the Uruguayan flag and later the *Solkbakken* of Norway; she was torpedoed and sunk by a submarine off Cape Finisterre on February 4, 1917. The *Horace*, *Canova* and *Cervantes* were all casualties of the First World War, while the *Cavour* survived until 1929 when delivered to shipbreakers.

Henderson's of Glasgow were to deliver another 'C' class ship in 1896, this being the much larger *Canning* of 5,366 gross tons which was to have quite an interesting career. She served the company well and during the Boer War was, together with the five later 'R' class ships, to serve the British Government as transports, particularly of horses and mules, to the war zone. In 1914 she was requisitioned by the Admiralty and became a Baloon ship—H.M.S.*Canning*, not returning to Lamport and Holt until 1919, for whom she traded for a further two years. In 1921 she passed to Greek owners as the *Okeanis*, and in 1924 became the *Arenzano*, and was broken up in 1925. The second ship delivered in 1896, also from Henderson's, was the smaller *Virgil* (3,338 gross tons) which remained in the fleet until broken up in Germany in 1924.

During 1896 George Holt died, having spent over fifty years engaged in the management of the business, during which he had seen it grow into one of the leading British Liner companies, and certainly had played a major part in the development of sea-borne trade with the East Coast of South America. Before his death his nephew George H. Melly, and Sidney Jones, a son of Charles W. Jones, together with Arthur Cook, joined the partnership.

Two ships appeared in 1898, the *Sallust* of 3,628 gross tons from the yard of Sir Raylton Dixon and Co. Ltd., and the *Raphael* of 5,855 gross tons from Henderson's. This 'R' class vessel was the first of five such ships to join the fleet in the next two years, all of varying sizes, but all being built specifically to carry cattle on the hoof from the Argentine to the United Kingdom. They provided much improved conditions for the transportation of such animals, and thereby greatly reduced the mortality rate amongst them during the voyage. Of these the *Sallust* was broken up in 1924, and the *Raphael* in 1930. The *Romney* and *Rembrandt* arrived in 1899, followed a year later by the *Raeburn* and *Rossetti*, the latter two being of some 6,500 gross tons, truly huge for those days. All came from Henderson's with the exception of the *Romney* which was delivered by Sir Raylton Dixon's yard. All survived into the late 1920s, when sold for breaking up.

Two 'C' class ships of 4,000 gross tons were delivered to the company in 1900 from the Belfast yard of Workman, Clark and Co. Ltd., and were named *Camoens* and *Calderon*. The former served until broken up in 1924, while the latter was lost on January 23, 1912 when she broke in two in the Crosby Channel, River Mersey, after a collision with the steamer *Muskateer*.

In 1901 came the delivery of a 'T' class ship of 4,343 gross tons, the *Thespis*, built by Dixon's. She was followed a year later by three sister-ships, the *Terence* from Henderson's, and the *Titian* and *Tintoretto* from Workman, Clark and Co. Ltd., Belfast. All were capable of a service speed of thirteen knots, which was very respectable for those days. Of these the *Thespis* and *Tintoretto* survived until broken up in 1930, but the other two were casualties of the First World War in 1917.

During 1901 three of the 'C' class vessels were transferred to the Belgian flag, the *Canova*, *Camoens* and *Calderon*, followed by the *Cervantes* in 1902, thus making up for disposals and transfers within the two fleets.

7. EXPANSION OF PASSENGER SERVICES

Lamport and Holt had, right from the start of the entry into the South American trade with steamers in 1863, carried a number of saloon passengers in their cargo ships, and had been engaged to some extent in the emigrant trade from Spain and Portugal to the South American Republics, carrying large numbers of steerage passengers. However, they now saw the greatest opportunities for the carriage of passengers as being on the run between South America and New York. In 1902 the Furness Withy company had found that two of their modern steamers, the *Evangeline* and *Loyalist*, both of 3,900 gross tons, and built by A. Stephen and Son Ltd., Glasgow in 1900 and 1901 respectively, were surplus to requirements. They were quickly taken over by Lamport and Holt and renamed *Tennyson* and *Byron*. Having more than the usual Lamport and Holt accommodation for passengers, they were pressed into service trading between New York and the River Plate, via Brazilian ports, carrying passengers and cargo, which when Northbound usually consisted of coffee.

This small venture into the passenger trade, helped by an ever increasing interest being paid to South America by the United States, was proving such a success (and that the company was in fact the major cargo carrier on this route) that orders were placed for the construction of three passenger liners equipped with refrigerated space, and with increased speed. They were the *Velasquez* of 7,542 gross tons delivered by Sir Raylton Dixon in 1906, and the *Veronese* (7,877 gross tons) and *Verdi* (7,120 gross tons) both delivered by Workman, Clark of Belfast in 1906 and 1907 respectively. Prior to the arrival of all three ships in the fleet an order was placed with D. and W. Henderson of Glasgow for another such liner, somewhat larger, but delivered later in 1907 as the *Voltaire*.

These ships quickly proved to be a great success with the travelling public, calls being made on their service between New York and the River Plate, at Salvador, Rio de Janeiro, Santos and the West Indies. They were tall, elegant ships and were the best in service on that route at the time. Meanwhile the *Tennyson* and *Byron* continued to be employed from New York, but rarely went further South than Santos. It was a truly fine venture by this now famous company, which had gathered an enviable reputation for itself.

However the service was not to be without incident, as on October 16, 1908, the *Velasquez* on a voyage Northbound from Buenos Aires to New York, via Brazil, ran aground on rocks between Ponta das Selas and Ponta das Maxilhoes, near Santos, during fog and high seas. Passengers took to the lifeboats where they remained until dawn, when all were put ashore on the beach called Praia dos Vellosos. Meanwhile the *Milton*, which arrived the same day at Santos from Antwerp, was despatched to search for her, and when located on October 17, the *Velasquez* was heeled over to starboard with her stern awash. The *Milton*, not having received any response to repeated blasts on her siren, commenced a search, and it was some time later that the passengers and crew were located on the beach. All were taken on board the *Milton*, together with the mails, and she returned to the *Velasquez*, where an attempt was made to salvage the passengers' baggage. High seas did not allow completion, so the *Milton* returned to Santos on the night of October 19-20. The *Velasquez* was quickly given up as a total loss, and all attempts at salvage abandoned and attendant tugs recalled. Fortunately there were no casualties amongst the passengers and crew.

A replacement quickly appeared a year later in the form of the *Vasari* of 10.117 gross tons from Workman, Clark and Co. Ltd., Belfast., and the service was back to normal.

Of these passenger ships, the *Tennyson* and *Byron* served the company until 1922 when they were disposed of to Chile. The *Veronese* was wrecked near Leixoes, Portugal on January 16, 1913, while on passage Liverpool to Buenos Aires, via Vigo and Leixoes, in very heavy seas. Of a total of 234 passengers and crew, twenty-seven persons were lost, due in part to the terrible weather which prevented the local lifeboat from assisting in the rescue. It was only possible to rescue the passengers and crew by means of a breeches buoy after the weather had subsided somewhat. Captain C. Turner was the last to leave. The *Voltaire* and *Verdi* were casualties of the First World War, while the *Vasari* alone survived, and was sold in 1928 becoming a Fish Factory ship named *Arctic Queen*. She passed to Russia in 1935 becoming the *Pishchevaya Industriya* and finally arrived at Kaohsiung for breaking up in 1979 after a remarkable seventy years afloat. In fact, having been deleted from Lloyds' Register decades earlier, through lack of information, it came as something of a surprise when she turned up at Hong Kong under her own steam en route to the breakers yard in Taiwan—for who in the West would believe that she had survived for so long.

During September, 1907 the *Raphael* struck a submerged rock off the coast of Chile, and to prevent her from sinking the master beached her, but the whole of her after deck was submerged. Eventually, after a large part of her cargo was jettisoned she was refloated a month later. Her starboard bilge had been damaged and her engines flooded. She was towed to Punta Arenas and after repairs subsequently continued her voyage to Le Havre, Swansea and Liverpool.

During this period no new cargo ships were added to the fleet, but a considerable amount of competition was encountered from various other shipping concerns, not least being that from the German companies. There was much rate cutting in an effort to fill one or other company's ships. This came to a head, and was handled in novel fashion by the partners in Lamport and Holt, when in a successful attempt to end this freight war a full cargo of coffee beans was transported to Hamburg from Santos *free of charge* aboard the *Veronese* in 1908, thereby bringing all the parties together to sort out each others' interests. This says much for the courage of those responsible for the direction of the company's affairs.

In 1908 the last four ships remaining under the Belgian flag were transferred back to the parent fleet, but Lamport and Holt continued to trade between Antwerp and South America, although the service took the form of a call on the East Coast of the United Kingdom service to Brazil and the River Plate.

There was an interesting development in 1908 when Lamport and Holt took a 49% share in a 5,394 gross ton steamer, built at Havre by Forges and Chantiers de la Mediteranee, to the order of E. Groses, Lamport and Holt's Le Havre agents for their monthly service to the West Coast of South America, who held 51% of the shares. She was duly completed as the *Colbert*, for service on this route, trading under the French flag, and the company held this interest in her until her loss through enemy action in 1917.

With the exception of the share in the French *Colbert*, it had now been nine years since a cargo ship had been added to the fleet. The intervening period had seen the start of Lamport and Holt's passenger services on a large scale, but in 1911 they acquired two ships which had been delivered the previous year to E.C. Thin and Company, from the Newcastle yard of Armstrong, Whitworth and Co. Ltd. These were the *Tremont* and *Tripoli*, both of 4,180 gross tons, which were renamed *Siddons* and *Spenser* respectively. The former was sold in 1923 and was ultimately broken up at Blyth in 1931, but the *Spenser* was to become a war loss in 1918.

Lamport and Holt now had four 'V' class passenger liners on the run between New York and the River Plate, and in addition the *Byron* and *Tennyson* were still serving the route as far South as Santos. Although most of the company's cargo liners trading from the United Kingtom to Brazil and the River Plate carried a limited number of first class passengers and large numbers of steerage passengers from both Portugal and Spain Southbound, it was decided by the management to commence a similar service from Liverpool to Brazil and the River Plate. So an order was placed with Workman, Clark and Co. Ltd., Belfast, for three additional 'V' class passenger liners, which were to have twin screws. The first appeared in 1911 as the *Vandyck* of 10,327 gross tons, followed the next year by the *Vauban* and *Vestris*. The last two had slightly larger passenger accommodation than their sister, being able to carry 280 first; 130 second and 200 third-class passengers, in real luxury.

However this service from Liverpool was to last but a short time, for in 1911 the Lamport and Holt partnership had become a public company under the title of Lamport and Holt Ltd., continuing to manage the ships which remained registered under the Liverpool, Brazil and River Plate Steam Navigation Co. Ltd. Messrs. George H. Melly and Arthur Cook became joint managing directors, but the Royal Mail Steam Packet Co. Ltd. was soon to take over control of the company, under the chairmanship of Owen Cosby Phillips, later to become Lord Kylsant. Lamport and Holt Ltd. became one of thirteen associate or subsidiary companies of the 'Kylsant Empire'. The following year, 1912, marked the departure of the company from Drury Buildings, Water Street, to the newly completed Royal Liver Building, on the Liverpool waterfront. Up until this time the two companies had run in competition with each other, and the appearance of three new and well found Lamport and Holt passenger liners between Liverpool and Brazil and the River Plate, did not fall in with the plans of Royal Mail at this time, who had three ships on order for their own service.

Thus it was that the Lamport and Holt ships were not to be allowed to run on this service for long. In fact while Royal Mail awaited the arrival of their new ships, two of the Lamport and Holt vessels were taken over for their service, the *Vandyck* making only a few such voyages alongside her sister *Vauban*. The latter served Royal Mail for much longer, and was renamed *Alcala* in April, 1913, but on delivery of the new tonnage to Royal Mail, reverted back to Lamport and Holt and her original name. All three ships were then transferred to Lamport and Holt's New York to Brazil and River Plate service, with calls at Trinidad and Barbados en route, thereby leaving the United Kingdom trade in the hands of the Royal Mail ships. However, the loss to the United Kingdom was to be the gain of the New York service, in that the three became the crack ships on the route with their 15 knot service speed. Accounting for the loss of the *Veronese* in 1913 this left six 'V' class liners and the smaller *Byron* and *Tennyson* on the route, a truly magnificent service which was the envy of all other lines engaged in the trade. They were without doubt the most popular liners, particularly with American passengers.

During this period a number of cargo ships joined the fleet. The *Dryden* was built to the company's order by William Hamilton and Co. Ltd., Port Glasgow, in 1912, remaining in the fleet until 1932 when sold to Greek operators. After passing through the hands of various owners under this flag she became a war loss, being sunk by air attack off Ostend on May 16, 1940.

During 1912 two ships were acquired from other owners. C. Barrie and Sons' *Den of Airlie* built by Russell and Co. Ltd., Port Glasgow the previous year, and the *Horley* from Houlder, Middleton and Company, which also dated from the previous year, but had been built by the

Northumberland Shipbuilding Co. Ltd., Newcastle. They were renamed *Archimedes* and *Euclid* respectively, and remained in the fleet for a number of years, both eventually going to the Ben Line. The *Archimedes* became the *Benmacdhui* in 1932 while the *Euclid* was renamed *Benvannoch* a year earlier. The former having been damaged by air attack off Yarmouth on February 10, 1941 was lost on December 21 the same year when sunk by a mine ten miles ENE of Spurn Head, while on passage from Immingham to Hong Kong with the loss of two of her crew. The *Euclid* was resold in 1936 to the Moller Line of Hong Kong, becoming the *Marie Moller*. On March 22, 1937 she was burnt out off Holyhead, while on passage India to Liverpool, becoming a constructive total loss, and was broken up at Troon later that year.

In 1913 three 'P' class and two 'S' class ships joined the fleet, of 5,600 and 4,900 gross tons respectively. The *Pascal*, *Phidias* and *Strabo* came from the yard of A. McMillan and Son, Dumbarton, while the *Plutarch* and *Socrates* came from Russell and Company, Port Glasgow. The *Pascal* was lost in the First World War, whilst the *Phidias* served the company until she was lost in the second conflict. The *Socrates* was sold in 1930, the *Plutarch* in 1931 and the *Strabo* a year later. The *Socrates* was torpedoed and sunk South West of Lands End on March 8, 1940 under the Greek flag, and the *Strabo*, having made her way through the Panamanian and Greek registers, found herself in 1938 under the Japanese flag. She became a war loss, being bombed and sunk by the United States Air Force on January 24, 1944 off Bougainville.

Of the five the *Plutarch* must have had the most eventful career. When sold in 1931 she went to Yugoslavia, becoming the *Durmitor*, surviving without mishap until she was captured on October 21, 1940 by the German armed raider *Atlantis* near Sunda Strait. A prize crew was put on board together with a number of Allied prisoners taken from earlier victims of the raider. She was sent to the French West African coast, but was in a sorry state long before her arrival, short of provisions and fresh water, and out of bunkers. Abandoned on her arrival, she was retaken in February, 1941 at Mogadishu by H.M.S. *Shropshire*, and placed under the British flag by the Ministry of War Transport, becoming the *Radwinter* in 1943. At the end of hostilities she was handed back to Yugoslavia in 1946. Reverting back to the name *Durmitor*, she traded under this flag until September 1963 when she arrived at Split for breaking up. She had clocked up a total of fifty years afloat, a clear testimonial to British Shipbuilding.

8. THE FIRST WORLD WAR

At the outbreak of the First World War the company owned a fleet of thirty-six steamers amounting to a total gross tonnage of 198,992, and during the period of hostilities eleven of these vessels were lost through enemy action, including three of the 'V' class passenger liners. In addition the ship under the French flag, in which Lamport and Holt held a 49% interest, was also lost.

First loss was the steamer *Cervantes* which was intercepted by the German light cruiser *Karlsruhe*, 100 miles South West of St. Paul's Rocks on October 8, 1914. After removing her crew the cruiser sank the *Cervantes* with explosive charges. The company's second loss represented another victim of this German cruiser some eighteen days later on October 26, when the *Vandyck* on passage from Buenos Aires to New York with over 200 passengers, mostly United States citizens, and a full cargo, including over 1,000 tons of frozen meat, was sighted by the cruiser. The *Vandyck* tried to escape but after a chase the cruiser caught and captured her just before noon, 690 miles West of St. Paul's Rocks. The passengers and crew were placed on the steamer *Asuncion*, which had previously broken out of Santos, with many other prisoners, and sent to Para (now known as Belem) which was reached on November 1. After removing much of her cargo, particularly the frozen meat, the cruiser sank the *Vandyck* the next day.

After these losses the company's fortunes held for a while, there not being any loss during the whole of 1915. However, during that year on December 8 the *Tintoretto* was attacked by a submarine 70 miles North West from Alexandria. During the attack the submarine fired torpedoes and used gunfire but fortunately missed, and the merchant ship responded by using her own gun, which was to effectively end the action, as the submarine withdrew.

But the following year things changed, and on February 9, 1916 the *Horace* was intercepted by the German raider *Moewe*, 600 miles North East of Pernambuco, and sunk. The next casualty was the *Voltaire* which fell victim to the *Moewe* on December 2, 1916, 650 miles West of the Fastnet. Fortunately in all these losses there had been no casualties on board the merchant ships. However, later in the same month the modern steamer *Pascal* was torpedoed and sunk by a submarine off the Casquets on December 17 with the loss of two lives. The master of the *Pascal* was taken prisoner by the submarine commander and was to spend the remainder of the war incarcerated in Germany.

On March 12, 1917 the *Raphael* was chased by a submarine off Southern Ireland, but used her superior speed to outrun the enemy vessel, before an attack could be launched. The *Terence* was the next Lamport and Holt vessel to be lost to the enemy when she was torpedoed and sunk on April 18, 1917, North West of the Fastnet, with the tragic loss of one life. Two days later the French *Colbert* was torpedoed and sunk in the Mediterranean.

The *Tintoretto* had a second lucky escape, when on July 1, 1917 a submarine fired a torpedo at her in the North Atlantic which fortunately missed. A week later, on July 8, the *Plutarch* had the same good fortune when a submarine torpedo missed her off the North West of Ireland. Again the company's luck held out when on August 21 a torpedo missed the liner *Vasari* in almost the same location.

The following day the liner *Verdi* was to be less fortunate as she fell victim to a German submarine which torpedoed and sank her 115 miles North West from Eagle Island Co. Mayo, Ireland, with the sad loss of six crew. Four days later on August 26 the *Titian*, sistership of the *Terence* lost four months earlier, was torpedoed and sunk South West of Malta. The *Memling*, only delivered to the company two years previously, and a fully refrigerated ship of the 'M' class, was torpedoed by a submarine off Brest on October 3, 1917, and with assistance made port, but was so badly damaged that she was found to be beyond repair, and was declared a constructive total loss, and broken up. On November 27, the *Herschel* survived a submarine attack in the Mediterranean when the torpedo fired at her missed. The last loss suffered in 1917 was the *Canova* which was torpedoed and sunk 15 miles South of Mine Head, Ireland on December 24 during which action seven members of the crew lost their lives.

Mr. Tom Waring served in a number of Lamport and Holt ships just prior to and during the First World War, and although his service was only short it is quite interesting, and therefore I give details.

> After leaving school in 1909 I worked for a time in the Manchester Ship Canal office at Latchford Locks, and noted that Lamport and Holt had a weekly sailing from New York to Manchester. In March, 1913 I went aboard the *Thespis* at Latchford and asked Captain Ferguson for a position as ordinary seaman, but she had already signed on so I was given a letter of introduction to the marine superintendent at Liverpool, Captain Bird.

> On the following Saturday, March 8, I sailed in the *Raeburn* as ordinary seaman for Brazil, calling at Leixoes where 350 emigrants were picked up, and after four months and ten days paid off with the princely sum of £5.9s.0d., all of thirty bob a month.

> I served aboard the *Raeburn* for a further four voyages, and during the last was on board at Buenos Aires when the Great War broke

out. The ship received orders to proceed to Santos where a number of German and Austrian ships were interned, having already been loaded with coffee destined for the United States.

Having arrived at Santos we became a radio link between the cruiser H.M.S. *Glasgow* and the British Consul. The German steamers *Santa Maria* and *Cap Ortegal* came alongside us (the *Raeburn*) and transferred their cargo to our holds, and it was clear that their crews were not very happy about it. Finally the cargo from the German steamer *Hockfels* was transferred. During this time the German steamer *Asuncion* went round the anchorage taking on coal, stores and men to supply the raiders *Karlsruhe* and *Cap Trafalgar*, and broke out on a Sunday night. We left for Rio de Janeiro, where cargo was taken on board from the Austrian *Laura* before proceeding via Pernambuco and Barbados to New Orleans where we arrived on October 3.

After discharge of the coffee, it had been intended that we were to be chartered to the British Government to transport horses and mules from Montreal to France; in the event these orders were changed and the ship was taken up by the French Government, and having grounded on a bank in the river while changing berths, we were towed off by the tug *W.C. Wilmot* on October 9.

Loading 900 mules and horses, we left for Bordeaux, with 75 cattlemen on board to tend the animals, arriving on October 28. This was the first cargo of horses and mules to arrive in France since the outbreak of war. A number of the crew were paid off here at their own request, and made their own way home, having been away for a fair time. As a result a part crew was signed on consisting of three French, one Japanese, one Spaniard, one American and a Swiss. I was promoted to quartermaster, and we left on November 5 for Newport News, passing and signalling St. Michaels, Azores on the 11th, arrived at Newport News on November 21.

Three days later the lamptrimmer broke his leg with the result that I was promoted to this position, the injured man being sent home on the *Raeburn's* sister *Romney*. Having loaded 910 horses we left on November 26 for Bordeaux, and after a rough passage arrived on December 10, to be diverted to La Pallice where we arrived the next day. During the passage we lost a total of fifty-two horses, which demonstrates the severity of the weather that we had encountered, and the extent to which these ships were loaded during the hostilities. On December 16 we left for Newport News, and again encountered bad weather; during December 20 we were hove to all day, losing the starboard lifeboat and accommodation ladder. On January 11, 1915 we arrived at Newport News and six days later left with 1,250 horses. On January 19, during very rough weather we lost most of the horses and pens from the foredeck.

Arriving at Bordeaux on February 5, we sailed again four days later, and after a fine passage arrived back at Newport News on February 24. On our arrival we discovered that the steamer *Anglo-Patagonian* had picked up our lifeboat which had been lost on December 20, and had feared the worst. After repairs we left again on March 14, arriving at Bordeaux on March 28. Leaving on April 1, we arrived at Newport News on April 16. After loading 1,250 horses we left on April 27 for St. Nazaire, arriving on May 11. Leaving four days later we arrived back at Newport News on June 1.

Having to wait a long time for a berth, we were informed that the next run was to Brest, hopefully to be paid off. We loaded 1,215 horses and sailed on June 30, arriving at Brest on July 14, where Captain Jardine was reluctant to pay us off. After discussions with the consul it was decided to despatch the *Raeburn* to Liverpool; sailing on July 18 we docked at Liverpool three days later, thereby ending a voyage which had lasted 14 months 10 days.

My next ship was Lamport and Holt's *Canova*. We sailed from Liverpool on August 14, 1915 for Brazil, via Lisbon, where we picked up emigrants for South America. After discharging in Brazil, the usual coffee cargo was loaded for New York, and we left, calling at the West Indies en route, discharging at Brooklyn. A large cargo was loaded, and we sailed for the United Kingdom on November 20; after encountering rough weather which necessitated heaving to for several days, we arrived in the Mersey on December 13, having been over 22 days on the passage, and it can well be imagined that there was much jubilation at Lamport and Holt's offices on our arrival at Eastham, en route to discharge at Manchester, as we had been more or less given up as lost.

My final voyage in a Lamport and Holt ship was aboard the *Siddons* from October 14, 1916 until January 6, 1917. The voyage was direct to Buenos Aires; Christmas Day 1916 being spent at Dakar waiting for a homeward convoy to form.

While engaged in the carriage of horses between the United States and France, the *Raphael*, on passage between Bordeaux and New Orleans in ballast in December 1914, was involved in the salvage of the *City of Lincoln* for which her crew were awarded salvage money.

The last loss suffered by the company during the war was the steamer *Spenser* which was torpedoed and sunk on January 6, 1918 off Bardsey Island in the Irish Sea, fortunately without loss of life. However a number

The full-rigged ship "Emma" was acquired by Lamport and Holt in 1847.
(Walker Art Gallery, Liverpool)

William James Lamport, 1815-1874.

George Holt, 1824-1896.

The steamer "Galileo" (1) of 1864.

Built in 1867 the "Tycho Brahe" was a product of A. Leslie and Company, Hebburn-on-Tyne.

The "Galileo" (2) of 1873 flying the Belgian flag, while owned by the subsidiary, Societe de Nav. Royale Belge Sud-Americaine, Antwerp.

(The Mariners Museum, Newport News)

The "Euclid" (1) was built in 1877 by Hall, Russell and Company, Aberdeen.
(The Mariners Museum, Newport News)

The ''Horrox'' of 1877 seen at New York.

The "Pliny" of 1878 was wrecked at New Jersey on May 13th, 1882.

(T. Rayner)

The "Lassell" (1) was built in 1879 by A. Leslie and Company, Hebburn-on-Tyne.
(The Mariners Museum, Newport News)

The "Nasmyth" (1) of 1880.

The "Mozart" of 1881.

The "Hogarth" (1) was built for Lamport and Holt in 1882.
(The Mariners Museum, Newport News)

The "Flaxman" of 1882 seen in the River Avon.

The "Amadeo" of 1884 was the pioneer vessel of the Argentine Steam Lighter Co. Ltd. She is seen in the Straits of Magellan, at San Gregorio, where she has lain beached since the 1930s.

(H. Matthews)

The "Garrick" of 1885.

The "Milton" was built in 1888 by D. & W. Henderson and Co. Ltd., Glasgow.

The "Canova" (2) of 1895 was torpedoed and sunk in 1917.

The "Horace" of 1895 fell victim to the German raider "Moewe" in 1916.

Dressed overall on the occasion of a Royal visit to the Mersey in 1913, the "Cavour" was built in 1895.

(T. Rayner)

The "Cervantes" (2) of 1895.

(World Ship Photo Library)

The steamship "Canning" (2) was built in 1896.

(T. Rayner)

The "Virgil" (1) of 1896.

Built in 1898 the "Sallust" (1) was a product of Sir Raylton Dixon and Co. Ltd., Middlesbrough.
(World Ship Photo Library)

The "Raphael" (1) of 1898 was built specifically to carry cattle on the hoof from Argentina. She is seen in sinking condition off the Chilean Coast in 1907, but was subsequently raised and repaired.

(T. Rayner)

TENNYSON.

Acquired in 1902 the "Tennyson" inaugurated a passenger service with her sister ship "Byron" (1) between New York, Brazil and the River Plate.

(T. Rayner)

The liner "Veronese" was built in 1906 for the New York, Brazil and River Plate Trade. She was wrecked in 1913.

(A. Duncan)

The "Vasari" of 1909 seen at New York.

(A. Duncan)

The "Vasari" was sold in 1928, but survived under the Russian flag until 1979, having had a remarkable career of seventy years.
(A. Duncan)

Built in 1911 the liner "Vandyck" (2) was a product of Workman, Clark and Co. Ltd., Belfast.

(T. Rayner)

The "Vandyck" was sunk in 1914 by the German cruiser "Karlsruhe".

(A. Duncan)

The "Vauban" of 1912 built for the New York, Brazil and River Plate trade.

(T. Rayner)

The "Vauban" of 1912.

(A. Duncan)

The liner "Vestris" of 1912 was lost in tragic circumstances in 1928.

(T. Rayner)

The "Archimedes" (2) joined the fleet in 1912.

(World Ship Photo Library)

Built in 1913 by A. McMillan and Son Ltd., Dumbarton, the "Pascal" (2) is seen on trials.

(T. Rayner)

The "Phidias" of 1913 served the Liverpool, Brazil and River Plate Steam Navigation Co. Ltd., for twenty-eight years, being a war loss in 1941.

(World Ship Photo Library)

The "Plutarch" of 1913.

(World Ship Photo Library)

The "Herschel" (3) of 1914 was laid up in the River Dart in the early 1930s.

The refrigerated cargo liner "Meissonier" was built in 1915.

The "Meissonier" seen on charter to Union Castle.

The "Murillo" (1) was one of six refrigerated ships built in the First World War for the Liverpool, Brazil and River Plate Steam Navigation Co. Ltd.

(A. Duncan)

The "Moliere" of 1916.

(A. Duncan)

Built in 1917 the "Millais" (1) is seen on charter to Union Castle.

(A. Duncan)

The "Millais" (1).

(World Ship Photo Library)

The "Biela" (2) was one of twelve steamers acquired from the British Government after the First World War.

(A. Duncan)

The "Biela" was torpedoed and sunk in 1942 with the loss of all hands.

(World Ship Photo Library)

The "Bronte" (1) of 1919.

(World Ship Photo Library)

The "Browning" (1) of 1919.

(A. Duncan)

The "Balfe" of 1919.

(A. Duncan)

The "Bonheur" of 1920.

(A. Duncan)

The "Balzac" (1) of 1920 laid up in the River Dart in the depression of the early 'thirties.

(World Ship Photo Library)

The "Boswell" of 1920.

(A. Duncan)

The steamer "Laplace" (2) of 1919 was the first ship built to the company's own order following the First World War.

(A. Duncan)

The "Lalande" (2) of 1920.

(World Ship Photo Library)

Built in 1921 the "Linnell" was the first motorship to enter the fleet.

(A. Duncan)

The motorship "Leighton" of 1921.

The "Hogarth" (2) and "Browning" (1) laid up on the outside of a tier of ships in the Dart during the depression of the early 1930s.
(World Ship Photo Library)

The passenger liner "Vandyck" (3) was built in 1921 by Workman, Clark and Co. Ltd., Belfast. She is seen in her cruising livery shortly before the Second World War.

(Stewart Bale Ltd.)

The passenger liner "Voltaire" (2) of 1923.

(Stewart Bale Ltd.)

The "Voltaire" of 1923.

The "Delius" was the first of seven 'D' class cargo liners built for Lamport and Holt Line Ltd., by Harland and Wolff Ltd., Belfast between 1937 and 1945. The ship is seen on trials.

(Harland and Wolff Ltd.)

The "Delius" of 1937.

(A. Duncan)

The "Delane" of 1938.

(A. Duncan)

of other ships were to survive enemy attacks. On January 26, 1918 the *Vestris* escaped when the torpedo aimed at her missed in the English Channel. The *Marconi* was torpedoed in the Mediterranean on February 27, with the tragic loss of two lives, but the ship remained afloat, reached port and was subsequently repaired. The *Meissonier* was shelled by a submarine West of Gibraltar on March 16, but managed to outrun the enemy vessel and escape. The *Dryden* struck a mine in the River Mersey on March 28 but managed to reach port where repairs were effected, and finally on August 27, 1918 the *Archimedes* evaded a torpedo in the English Channel.

Mr. Frank Evans served in the steamer *Herschel* for about two years during the war as a Naval Gunner, and his recollections are of interest.

I joined the *Herschel* at Liverpool early in 1917, having been sent up from Plymouth to join as a naval gunner. The ship had not been docked long, when to my utter amazement I noted on an elevated platform aft an imitation gun, made of wood by the 'Chippy'. It was removed and a 4.7in. Vickers gun was installed, and a full gun crew placed on board. The *Herschel* was evidently built for the Spanish passenger traffic because all the cabins were lettered in Spanish.

Leaving Liverpool at night we took on a full cargo of coal at Newport, Mon., for Port Said, and on joining a convoy at Avonmouth, set off for Port Said under the command of Captain Frodson. Having discharged, we moved to Alexandria where a full cargo of cotton was loaded for Boston (USA), where we arrived about three weeks later. Then light ship to Newport News where a cargo of coal was taken on board for Buenos Aires, for the Argentine Railway. I noted a large amount of German tonnage in port at Buenos Aires, due to the presence outside of the cruisers *Gloucester* and *Bristol*. We loaded a cargo of corned beef, linseed, Indian corn and hides, then crossed the River Plate to Montevideo where we completed with bagged wheat before setting out for Liverpool. On our way home we were in action with a submarine on the surface in the area of the Gulf of Mexico, and again with another in the Bay of Biscay, but fortunately survived both attacks, to arrive safely at Barry, eventually steaming round to Liverpool for discharge.

Our next voyage was under the command of Captain Carey, from Liverpool to Durban, via Suez, thence to Buenos Aires, where we stayed three weeks, leaving part loaded for Rio de Janeiro to take on bagged wheat. Thence to Bahia for completion with coffee, arriving at Liverpool after the armistice had been signed.

In the early part of the war most regular services were maintained, but towards the end it was found increasingly difficult to maintain the New York to South America service, it having to be reduced considerably.

The following figures produced by the company relate to the cargo carried by the *Archimedes* alone during the period of hostilities. She was employed throughout on carrying stores, etc., between the United Kingdom and France, and carried over 145,000 troops, 70,000 horses, 225,000 bags of mail, 12,000 vehicles, and a further 68,320 tons of stores and materials. During this period 351,000 tons of meat was carried in the company's refrigerated steamers to the armies in France and elsewhere.

As well as the 'R' class being used on carrying horses and mules across the Western Ocean to France, a number of other Lamport and Holt vessels were engaged in this service, and others were used for carrying stores for the armed forces to all theatres of the war. The *Tintoretto* was so employed on the route from Quebec and Montreal to France with such materials, and was later to be found with other units of the fleet carrying horses from Newport News to Salonica. During the whole period of the war, the *Canning* was used by the Admiralty as a balloon ship.

A number of ships joined the fleet during the war, having been built to the company's own order. There were the two 'H' class ships, the *Herschel* already mentioned, and *Holbein* of 6,200 gross tons, delivered by D. and W. Henderson and Co. Ltd., Glasgow, in 1914 and 1915 respectively. However the *Herschel* was in the hands of the Admiralty from June to September, 1914.

It is interesting to note that Lamport and Holt had been carrying frozen meat since a contract was obtained to carry 230 tons a month in 1886, the first ship being fitted with refrigerated space being the *Thales* in 1887.

Six fully refrigerated ships were built for Lamport and Holt between 1915 and 1917, designated the 'M' class; they were easily recognised by their huge funnel which stood some 66 feet above the boat deck. Of these, four were sisterships in the full sense of the word, being twin-screw vessels. the *Meissonier, Murillo, Moliere* and *Marconi*. The first three came from the yard of Russell and Co. Ltd., Port Glasgow and were 7,206 gross tons, while the *Marconi* of 7,402 gross tons was delivered by Harland and Wolff Ltd., Glasgow, who also built the single screw *Millais*. The sixth, but first to enter service, was the *Memling* from A. McMillan and Co. Ltd., Dumbarton, previously mentioned as a war loss. The other five survived the war, and were employed on the frozen and chilled meat trade from the Argentine to London, a contract being signed with Weddel and Company. In 1929-30 the *Meissonier, Murillo* and *Moliere* were sold to H. and W. Nelson Ltd., of London, for whom they continued trading to the River Plate. All three passed to the Royal Mail fleet in 1932 together with the rest of the Nelson fleet, the latter two being renamed *Nalon* and *Nela* respectively. The *Meissonier* was renamed *Nasina* the following year, and was sold to an Italian firm two years later, she became a war loss when torpedoed and sunk by H.M.S. *Unshaken* off Brindisi on August 11, 1943. The other two continued to serve Royal Mail until the *Nalon* (ex *Murillo*) was bombed and sunk West of Ireland, while homeward bound from Cape Town on November 6, 1940. The *Nela* (ex *Moliere*) lasted until sold to be broken up in 1946 at Ghent. The *Marconi* was sold to Kaye, Son and Co. Ltd., London, in 1937, and was lost on May 21, 1941 when torpedoed and sunk South East of Cape Farewell in convoy, there being a heavy loss of life. The *Millais* was sold to the Blue Star Line in 1938, becoming their *Scottish Star*, she was torpedoed and sunk on February 20, 1941 East of Barbados, on passage Liverpool to Montevideo.

The *Swinburne* and *Sheridan* were the last two vessels delivered to the company during the war years; joining in 1917 they were both of 4,600 gross tons. The former became a Second World War loss, while the *Sheridan* was to stay in the fleet for some thirty years, mostly employed on the New York, Brazil and River Plate service until sold in 1947.

Captain B.S. Haikney joined the company as far back as August 1917, having spent one voyage in the *Veronese* as an ordinary seaman in 1908, and served at first as third officer aboard the *Camoens* which was capable of 14 knots.

As she was quite a fast ship, we proceeded South in convoy to Dakar, and then unescorted to the River Plate, where grain was loaded, a call being made at Recife homeward to complete with sugar, arriving at Liverpool on December 15, 1917.

Then followed two trips in the *Tennyson* between Manchester and New York, outwards light ship, and homewards in convoy with foodstuffs. The *Tennyson* being the naval commander's ship, she carried a naval signalling staff on board.

In June, 1918 I joined the liner *Vestris* at Southampton as second officer, and after a passage Westbound, in August left New York with 800 nurses and stenographers for Le Havre. During the passage an outbreak of 'Spanish Flu' occurred, causing the deaths of eight of these women, and laying most on board low. After our arrival at Le Havre we proceeded to Dartmouth where most of the crew were changed, and we provisioned and bunkered for the next voyage. Early in the morning of November 11, 1918 while sailing out of Dartmouth, we received a semaphore signal from the Admiralty Office, Dartmouth, as follows:- 'To Master *Vestris*, hostilities will cease at 11am GMT today, November 11, 1918. You will proceed on your voyage burning navigation lights, avoiding all traffic as much as possible, and cease zig-zagging. Report immediately any suspicious vessel to nearest radio station.' As can be imagined this caused a great deal of jubilation on board, and more still when two German submarines were sighted under a Royal Navy escort.

Lamport and Holt Ltd. was still a part of the Royal Mail Group, and in common with other members of the group had shares in a number of shipping ventures of a local nature in South America. Perhaps the most important of these was the large holding acquired in the Nicholas Mihanovich flotilla in December, 1917. This concern operated a large fleet of tugs at Buenos Aires and La Plata, and cargo and passenger services throughout the River Plate, even as far North as Asuncion in Paraguay. A number of the tugs in this fleet were painted in the Lamport and Holt funnel colours, and it is interesting to note that a tug which was in the fleet some time before these shares were acquired had the name *Lamport*. She still survived in the 1970s under different owners, but carrying the same name.

9. THE DEPRESSION AND LAMPORT AND HOLT LINE LTD.

After the war the company began to acquire new tonnage, principally ships of the standard types built towards the end of hostilities, a large number of which had been managed by the company on behalf of the Shipping Controller. These were to fall into three classes. Two steamers of 6,500 gross tons ordered by the Shipping Controller were completed for Lamport and Holt as the *Nasmyth* and *Newton*. The former was broken up in 1938, while the *Newton* had been sold in 1933 becoming the Greek *Mount Othrys*, and was lost on January 6, 1945 in a collision in the River Thames on passage St. John, New Brunswick to London with grain. She was so badly damaged that she was declared a constructive total loss and broken up. A Japanese built steamer of 7,000 gross tons built in 1917 became the *Delambre* and served the company mostly from the United Kingdom until she became a war loss in 1940.

Nine standard ships of 5,300 gross tons each were acquired during 1919 and 1920, some straight from the builders, others having helped in the war effort; they became the 'B' class and were named—*Bernini*, *Boswell*, *Balfe*, *Biela*, *Bruyere*, *Bronte*, *Balzac*, *Browning* and *Bonheur*. The *Bernini* and *Boswell* were sold in 1933, but the remaining seven ships were in the fleet until the Second World War. Only one survived this second period of hostilities, six being lost through enemy action. The sole survivor was the *Balfe* which was not sold until 1950, and was eventually broken up in 1959.

Having acquired twelve steamers from the Shipping Controller the fleet was more like its former size, but it was also felt that a new class should be laid down to the company's own order, and in consequence two steamers were delivered, designated the 'L' class. They were the *Laplace* and *Lalande* of about 7,000 gross tons, delivered in 1919 and 1920 respectively, from the yards of A. McMillan and Sons Ltd., Dumbarton, and D. and W. Henderson and Co. Ltd., Glasgow. The former was to become a war loss in 1942, while the latter remained in the fleet until sold in 1951.

Having taken delivery of these two 'L' class steamers, the company, ever looking to make improvements, placed an order for three twin-screw motorships with A. McMillan and Co. Ltd. They were the first such ships to be ordered by the company, and were of the same tonnage and basic appearance as the previous two steamers. The *Linnell* and *Leighton* joined the fleet in 1921, followed a year later by the *Lassell*. They proved highly successful in service. The *Linnell* having stranded at Alexandria in 1939 was found to be so badly damaged that on her return to the United Kingdom she was sold for breaking up, arriving at Troon on August 23, 1939. The *Leighton* survived the war and having been sold for breaking up in 1946, was subsequently resold, and finally scuttled in the North Atlantic with a gas bomb cargo in the following year. The *Lassell* was to become a war loss in 1941. During 1921 an 8,100 gross ton steamer, the *Hogarth*, arrived from Henderson's shipyard and remained in the company's service until broken up in 1933 at Port Glasgow.

On the passenger liner side, the old faithfuls, *Tennyson* and *Byron* both survived the war, together with the *Vasari*, *Vauban* and *Vestris*. The latter three resumed their service from New York in 1919, but initially they commenced a charter to Cunard taking passengers and cargo Westbound from Liverpool to New York, and then for their owners' account going South to Buenos Aires, and returning to the United Kingdom with frozen meat from the River Plate. After about six Atlantic crossings for Cunard they resumed their service back and forth from New York to the River Plate, via Brazil, Barbados and Trinidad. In 1922 the *Vauban* and *Vestris*, together with the later *Vandyck*, made a single Westbound crossing from Hamburg to New York on charter to Royal Mail, but after this they resumed their normal sailings.

During August, 1919 when Southbound from New York to Buenos Aires with passengers, a fire was discovered in the No. 3 cross-bunker of the *Vestris*, and after smothering the bunker as much as possible, H.M.S. *Dartmouth*, cruising in the vicinity, was called to assist. She accompanied the *Vestris* to St. Lucia, where about 600 American passengers were disembarked, and housed in the barracks ashore, food being conveyed from ship to shore four times a day, it taking about ten days to extinguish the fire. After this she resumed her voyage South to the River Plate, and took a full cargo of frozen meat home to the United Kingdom.

Having lost three 'V' class passenger liners in the war, there was a gap which Lamport and Holt had to fill, and as a result they ordered two twin-screw steamers from the Belfast yard of Workman, Clark and Co. Ltd. The first of these, the *Vandyck* of 13,233 gross tons, was launched on February 24, 1921, and had five holds for refrigerated and general cargo, and accommodation for 300 first, 150 second and 230 third class passengers. The first class comprised one, two and three berth cabins, and included a number of special cabins with private bathroom, toilet and extra storage space. Her sistership, *Voltaire* of 13,248 gross tons, was launched on August 14, 1923, and joined the fleet later that year.

The *Tennyson* and *Byron*, now somewhat surplus to requirements, and somewhat aged, were disposed of, and with the arrival of the *Voltaire*, the passenger fleet trading from New York was brought up to five ships, thereby allowing a fortnightly service on the route. The two new ships proved to be very popular with passengers, and so they ought, providing, as they did, a new standard in accommodation. It is worthy of note that Madam Pavlova and her corps-de-ballet and Shackleton of Arctic fame, both travelled aboard the *Vandyck* in her early days on the service.

On October 25, 1927 the *Rossetti* under the command of Captain W. Denson, who had joined the company in 1908, went to the assistance of the *Principessa Mafalda*, which was in distress off the Brazilian coast, and when this ship sank assisted in the rescue of passengers and crew, for which Captain Denson received a Gold Medal from the Italian Chamber of Commerce. During the following year the *Vasari* was sold.

On November 10, 1928, the *Vestris*, having left New York for Barbados and Buenos Aires under the command of Captain W. J. Carey with 129 passengers and 197 crew, encountered heavy weather the next day, and on the evening of that day was struck by waves of exceptional size and force, flooding the boat deck, and amongst other damage washed two lifeboats away. Part of her cargo and bunker coal shifted, and as a result she took on a heavy list to starboard, from which she was unable to recover, the pumps being unable to cope. By the following day the ship was in a bad way, and having failed to right her Captain Carey sent out a distress message. The ship quickly increased her list, and had to be abandoned about 300 miles off Hampton Roads, sinking at 2 pm. Lifeboats were picked up by the steamers *American Shipper*, *Miriam* and *Berlin*, and by the United States battleship *Wyoming*. Captain Carey was among the 112 passengers and crew lost.

After this tragedy, a fair amount of adverse publicity was encountered, and, with the depression fast setting in, the service from New York by the passenger liners was discontinued, and the three remaining ships were brought home to be laid-up, the *Vauban* and *Vandyck* at Southampton and the *Voltaire* in the River Blackwater.

The recession was now upon the world, and to add to this the 'Kylsant Empire' became enmeshed in a complete financial crash. As a result Lamport and Holt Ltd. was placed in the hands of a Receiver, who tried to save as much as possible of its assets. Most of Lamport and Holt's foreign interests were quickly disposed of, the Mihanovich shares being sold in September, 1930.

In January, 1930 Lamport and Holt owned a fleet of forty-one ships, of which three were passenger liners. Gradually as the depression got worse and the amount of cargo available for shipment got less, the majority of the fleet was sent to lay-up berths on their arrival back in the United Kingdom. Of these forty-one ships, almost half were disposed of between 1930 and 1935, as follows:—

Year	Broken up	Sold for further trading	Total
1930	Raphael, Thespis and and Tintoretto	Meissonier, Murillo, Moliere and Socrates	7
1931	Raeburn	Euclid and Plutarch	3
1932	Vauban	Dryden, Archimedes and Strabo	4
1933	Hogarth	Newton, Bernini and Boswell	4
1934	Herschel	—	1
1935	Holbein	—	1

Of the remaining ships, in the early 'thirties there were very few actually trading, many other units being laid-up. Considering the size of the fleet prior to the 'Kylsant Crash', and the large number of men who had been dependent on the company for a livelihood, it was a further tragedy in itself, as suddenly men who had been with them for years were now unemployed, or forced to be demoted. Masters were sailing as chief officers or in some cases even lower rank. It was a sorry state indeed and, in an effort to improve matters for these men, the company fitted out the *Lassell* to be wholly manned by officers and engineers, this in an effort to keep loyal men until better days. It was not unusual to see men qualified as master and chief engineer sailing as ratings, and this situation was by no means confined to the Lamport and Holt fleet, but was widespread at that time.

To illustrate this I have reproduced details of some personal recollections.

Captain B.S. Haikney

I had been serving as chief officer for eight years when I arrived at Liverpool aboard the *Balfe* in May, 1932, and after discharging her cargo we took her round to the River Blackwater, where the *Bernini* and *Boswell* had been laid-up for some considerable time. I served aboard the *Balfe* at this lay-up berth for two-and-a-half years rusticating on half pay, until at my own request I was relieved in November, 1934, to become second officer aboard the *Lassell*, which was manned entirely by officers. It was to be another two years before I was able to revert back to chief officer.

Captain B. M. Metcalf

I had joined the company in May 1924 as an ordinary seaman, and having qualified to second mate early in 1930 was offered the post of third officer in one of the ships on the New York—South

56

American run. I was to have served as a Cadet aboard a ship outward until I joined this ship. Meanwhile the crash came and the marine superintendent—Captain Richardson wrote to me, regrettably withdrawing this appointment, but offered me instead the post of A.B. aboard the *Holbein* instead. This I readily accepted, and after two voyages joined the *Lassell*, that work horse for all officers. After one disastrous voyage, when an epidemic of typhoid broke out, and two members of the crew died, I left the ship in a sorry state, and after a period of convalescing joined the *Voltaire* in 1932, which was starting her series of successful cruises, sailing for one voyage as quartermaster. I was then offered the third mate's post in the *Sheridan* on the New York service, where I stayed three instead of the customary two years.

Captain D. C. Roberts

I joined Lamport and Holt in March 1915, having served previously in sailing ships, and was in possession of my extra master's certificate—square rigged. I joined the *Pascal* as second officer, and gained my first command in May, 1925 when I was appointed master of the *Raphael*. I commanded a number of vessels until arriving home in the *Bruyere* after the collapse of the Royal Mail group, I had to revert back to the rank of chief officer. It was to be just before the Second World War before I was re-appointed master, joining the *Sheridan* at New York.

During the spring of 1932 the *Voltaire* and *Vandyck* were brought out of lay-up, and were made ready for a series of cruises from Southampton and Liverpool, and these proved so successful that they were specially fitted for this purpose. Their hulls were painted white, and from then until just before the Second World War they were so employed, cruising to the Mediterranean, Atlantic Islands, West African ports, West Indies, Norwegian Fjords and Baltic ports. It was at this time, in recognition of the trade and employment brought by the company to the Port of Liverpool, that Lamport and Holt were presented with the City of Liverpool's colours, and to this day is the only shipping company privileged to fly the Liverpool civic flag at the jackstaff of its ships when moored in any port in the world.

The general manager from 1924 to 1930 had been Mr. Alfred Woods, but in 1930 he was succeeded by Mr. Francis H. Lowe, who was to manage the company through its most difficult period, during the Receivership. In the middle of 1934, the Liverpool, Brazil and River Plate Steam Navigation Co. Ltd. took over all the assets of Lamport and Holt Ltd. and was reborn under the new title of Lamport and Holt Line Ltd. A new board of directors was formed as follows: Philip Edward Haldin (chairman), Alfred Woods (deputy chairman), Francis Hugh Lowe (managing director), Philip Runciman, Charles Frederick Holland and William Alexander Young.

It will be remembered that the last ship to enter the fleet was the passenger liner *Voltaire* of 1923, but that the last cargo ship acquired was the *Lassell* of 1922, third of the series of motorships built by A. McMillan and Son Ltd., Dumbarton. Such were the company's fortunes under the new board of directors, that in 1937 the first of an order for three new motorships appeared from the Belfast yard of Harland and Wolff Ltd., and became the 'D' class, causing quite a stir in shipping circles when they appeared due to their revolutionary profile. They were streamlined, and something of a departure from the normal appearance of a cargo liner. The funnel was incorporated into the superstructure, and housed a small part of the accommodation. Like the 'L' class before them, they were fitted for carrying twelve passengers in comfortable accommodation, and were originally designed for the company's route from Glasgow and Liverpool to the River Plate. The first ship was the *Delius*, followed in 1938 by the *Delane* and *Devis*, all open shelter deck vessels of some 6,000 gross tons. They were fitted with a double-acting 6-cylinder two-stroke oil engine built and installed by the builders. They took the place of older ships in the fleet, the *Delius* replacing the *Marconi*, the *Delane* and *Devis* replacing the *Millais* and *Nasmyth*.

10. THE SECOND WORLD WAR

At the outbreak of the Second World War the fleet consisted of twenty-one ships of which fourteen were to be lost during the period of hostilities, including the two last passenger liners, *Vandyck* and *Voltaire*, whilst on service with the Royal Navy.

Owing to the threat of hostilities all cruising ceased and the *Voltaire* and *Vandyck* were quickly converted for the carriage of troops. In June, 1939 the *Voltaire* sailed for Bombay with troops carrying homewards a number of NCO's and their families. While passing through the Bay of Biscay an Admiralty 'A' message was received warning that hostilities were imminent. Arriving at Southampton on August 28, she disembarked her passengers, and, the crew not being allowed ashore, the ship was painted grey overall and the following evening sailed for Scapa Flow.

At Scapa the *Voltaire* served as a hostel ship for the services, and was anchored close to H.M.S. *Iron Duke*. She was there when war was declared and when H.M.S. *Royal Oak* was sunk, and on the morning after this last event was present when German aircraft made an attack on H.M.S. *Iron Duke*. Although one of the aircraft was shot down a hit was scored on the *Iron Duke* which necessitated her having to be beached. The *Voltaire* at this time had all the survivors from the *Royal Oak* on board, and the master, expecting another attack, wisely put these ashore at Flotta Island until nightfall. Hardly had this been carried out, when another air attack commenced, the *Voltaire* being the target on this occasion, and although a number of near misses were registered, and a small amount of damage was caused to the ship, she survived the experience. The following day the *Voltaire* was renamed *Iron Duke II*, replacing the original.

At the end of October 1939 the *Iron Duke II* (*Voltaire*) sailed from Scapa Flow for Newcastle. There at the yard of Swan Hunter and Wigham Richardson Ltd. she was refitted and converted into an armed merchant cruiser. Her main armament comprised eight-6 inch breech loading guns, which came from the old H.M.S. *Tiger* of Jutland fame. Most of the peacetime officers, at the request of Lamport and Holt, stayed with the ship, which had now become H.M.S. *Voltaire*.

In January 1940 she sailed for Malta, where she was on contraband control, with an area of patrol from the Adriatic Eastwards to the Dardanelles. After being employed on such duties, she left the Mediterranean in June 1940, and was then employed escorting convoys across the North Atlantic, mainly from Halifax, but on occasions from Bermuda. It was while so employed that the *Voltaire* was lost. She had left Halifax, Nova Scotia, had called at Trinidad, and was en route to Freetown for a convoy, when in the early morning of April 9, 1941 she fell in with the German armed raider *Thor*, and after a heavy battle, was sunk by the superior gunfire of the German vessel. A total of 197 survivors were picked up by the raider, all of which were to spend the remainder of the war as prisoners in Germany.

Shortly after the outbreak of war the *Vandyck* was taken over by the Admiralty, and was converted to an armed boarding vessel—H.M.S. *Vandyck*. She was to survive until June 10, 1940, when en route to take part in the evacuation of troops from Norway, she was bombed and sunk by an enemy aircraft off the Norwegian coast, while under the command of Captain G. F. W. Wilson, RN. Two officers and five ratings were lost; 29 officers and 132 ratings having landed, were taken prisoner by the Germans and were to be incarcerated in Germany for the remainder of the war.

Having dealt with the loss of the two passenger ships on service with the Royal Navy, we come to the losses suffered by the ships left on service with the company. The first casualty suffered by Lamport and Holt was the *Bronte* which was torpedoed by the German submarine *U34* in home waters on October 27, 1939, outward bound for South America, with a crew of forty and one passenger, a 71 year old inventor, fortunately without loss of life. The *Bronte* remained afloat for some time, and having at first been abandoned, some of the crew were put back on board in an attempt to tow the ship into port. However, these efforts were thwarted by the bad weather, and eventually three days later she was sunk by a charge set by her escort. Captain S. Dickinson, who was to become the cargo superintendent at Liverpool, was serving as third officer in the *Bronte* at the time.

On April 27, 1940 the *Delius* was damaged by an air attack whilst lying at Romsdalsfjord, Norway, a direct hit being recorded. This attack was to last two days.

On July 7, of the same year, the *Delambre* was proceeding homeward from South America to join a convoy at Freetown, when she was intercepted by the German raider *Thor*, which was later to account for the loss of the *Voltaire*. After a two hour chase by the raider, the much slower *Delambre* was overhauled and forced to stop. (Captain Pratt of the *Delambre* was captured in similar fashion by the raider *Moewe* in the earlier war.) After transferring the crew to the raider, the *Delambre* was sunk. The crew were to remain in the raider for some time, before being transferred to an auxiliary, which was to land them in occupied territory. The late Hugh Binney, well remembered at Lamport and Holt, was serving as ship's carpenter at the time, and he related how he left his home on May 6, 1940, not arriving back until exactly five years to the day, having spent most of the intervening period as a prisoner of war in Germany.

On October 15, 1940 the *Bonheur* was torpedoed and sunk by the submarine *U138* while outward bound in convoy, Liverpool to Rosario, the sinking taking place in home waters. The following month, on November 18, the *Biela* was damaged by an aircraft attack in position 52.26′N, 16.31′W; and on the night of December 20/21, the *Laplace* was damaged by a bomb while lying at Liverpool. On February 26, 1941 the *Swinburne* was bombed and sunk by German aircraft in home waters. On April 6, the same year the *Devis* was damaged by an air attack while lying at Piraeus.

During 1940 two further 'D' class ships were added to the fleet, the *Debrett* and *Defoe*, both coming, like their earlier sisters, from Harland and Wolff Ltd., Belfast. There were now five of this class trading for the company.

The next loss was the *Lassell* which, having left Liverpool for South America under the command of Captain A. R. Bibby early in April 1941, was torpedoed on the evening of April 30, about 300 miles South West of the Cape Verde Islands. I quote hereunder the report made by the chief officer to the owners on his return to the United Kingdom, in full, as it is an interesting account of the loss and subsequent journey in one of the lifeboats.

M.V. Lassell

Account of the loss through enemy action, and log of the survivors in No. 3 Boat.

H. W. Underhill—Chief Officer
D. Enticknap—3rd Officer

Wednesday, April 30, 1941

Noon—In position latitude 13.55′North, longitude 28.59′West True course S 7 E. Speed 10.2 knots. Moderate NE breeze. Slight sea and moderate NE swell. Cloudy, fine and clear.

18.02—In position latitude 12.55′North, longitude 28.50′West. The vessel was struck by a torpedo on the port side in the engine room near No. 4 bulkhead. No. 4 boat was smashed and thrown inboard. All W/T gear rendered useless. Both engines stopped instantly and the engine room flooded. The vessel listed about 10 degrees to port and returned to an even keel almost immediately. She then commenced to settle by the stern, and the abandon ship signal was given. No. 2 boat was lowered, but, owing to the vessel's way and the effect of the swell, was damaged against the ship's side and had to be abandoned. Nos. 1 and 3 boats were lowered and manned, although the work was rendered difficult by quantities of fuel oil and sheep dip which were forced by the air pressure out of the engine room and No. 4 hold ventilators onto the boat deck.

18.08—No. 3 boat with the 3rd officer in charge, cleared the ship with twenty men.

18.09—No. 1 boat with Captain Bibby in charge, cleared the ship with chief and 2nd officers, twenty-six men and one lady passenger.

18.10—The vessel foundered stern first at an angle of approximately 60 deg. The mainmast crumpled and fell to the deck as she went under. A quantity of flotsam, including a number of rafts, and a pedigree bull floated clear.

18.15—A very large submarine marked *U22* (although it has been confirmed that it was *U107* which was responsible for the loss of the vessel) surfaced about three hundred yards from the boats and opened fire with machine guns on the bull which was struggling in the water. Both boats lay to.

18.20—The submarine dived. No. 3 boat pulled to the wreckage of No. 2 boat and salvaged one case corned beef, two cases condensed milk and two casks water.

18.45—Night fell, both boats laying to sea anchors and maintained communication by flashing torches.

Thursday, May 1

At 05.00 No. 3 boat pulled to No. 1 boat half-a-mile distant. Chief Officer Underhill and four men were transferred from No. 1 boat. It was then definitely established that only two men missing were 3rd. Engineer J. Chaney and Greaser W. Quinn. As both these men were in the engine room at the time the torpedo struck the ship they were assumed to have been trapped by the inrush of water and drowned.

Both boats lay to sea anchors throughout the day and No. 1 boat used the portable radio transmitter at two-hourly intervals.

At 16.00 a large unidentified steamer was sighted about four miles off to the eastward. The radio transmitter was used, and No. 3 boat burned two red flares. The vessel maintained her course to the northward and passed from sight. The first ration of water and biscuits was issued in No. 3 boat at 18.00.

Both boats lay to sea anchors as on the previous night.

Friday, May 2.

No. 3 boat pulled over to No. 1 boat at daylight and reported to Captain Bibby for orders. One 7 gallon cask of fresh water was transferred to No. 1 boat. Both boats lay to until 08.00 when sails were hoisted and course set to NE x E true (E x E magnetic) in an endeavour to reach the Cape Verde Islands. This was found to be impossible, and No. 3 boat, sailing as close to the wind as she could, made SE x E true.

No. 1 boat seemed to be sailing a little closer to the wind, but both boats made a great deal of leeway.

At 11.00 the top gudgeon on the stern post of No. 3 boat carried away, rendering the rudder useless. This was therefore jettisoned and the sweep oar rigged as a jury rudder and served fairly satisfactorily.

At 16.00 No. 3 boat, when about three miles ahead of No. 1 hove to, to enable her to close before nightfall. No. 1 boat maintained her course and passed to windward. No. 3 reset her sails and proceeded.

Communication was established, but at 23.00 No. 3 boat failed to receive any answer to her signals, and although the torch was used at frequent intervals the two boats never regained touch.

Saturday, May 3.

From here on this account is written as the Log Book of No. 3 boat alone.

As we were now alone we decided to take stock of our resources and come to some definite organisation and routine.

The following is a list of the boat's personnel:

Name	*Rank*
H. W. Underhill	Chief Officer
D. Enticknap	3rd officer
A. B. Withers	6th engineer
J. Simpson	7th engineer
H. Hutton	3rd radio officer
P. J. Guy	Cadet
K. Elgin	Cadet
G. Robinson	AB
J. Blundell	AB
J. Graham	AB
J. Quinn	AB
D. Leicester	OS
W. Parry	OS
H. Scott	Deck boy
J. Sullivan	Greaser
T. Wake	2nd steward
E. McArdle	Assistant steward
A. Buck	Steward's boy

Name	Rank
W. Childs	Private, R.M.
J. Allingham	Seaman Gunner
F. H. Butler	Bombardier, R.A.
W. Wilkinson	Gunner, R.A.
P. Giffard	Gunner, R.A.
H. Bolch	Gunner, R.A.
J. Holmes	Gunner, R.A.
T. Caddy	Gunner, R.A.

The crew were divided into three sections. Six men living in the bow of the boat were made responsible for the lookout at night. The seventeen men amidships kept the day lookout and bailed whenever necessary (usually twice a day). The chief and 3rd officers and A.B. Robinson kept two-hour watches at the steering oar. 6th engineer Withers, having been badly burned on the left arm and side by blazing fuel oil in the engine room, was exempted from all duties.

The stores were checked over, and the following list drawn up. This includes the boat's own stores and those salvaged from No. 2 boat:

24 gallons fresh water in one 10 gallon and two 7 gallon casks.
112 lbs biscuits in two airtight containers.
72 lbs Nestles sweetened condensed milk in 1 lb tins.
120 lbs Armour's corned beef in forty-eight 1 kilo tins.
500 Gold Flake cigarettes in ten tins of 50.
20 lifeboat matches in watertight container.
One First Aid outfit.
12 blankets.
24 Regulation red flares (two of these were used yesterday).

Apart from this list there was the usual lifeboat equipment specified by the Ministry of Shipping and a number of cigarettes and matches in the private possession of various members of the crew. This seemed a fairly satisfactory list of provisions, and the only question which gave rise to any anxiety was that of matches. It was decided not to pool them, but orders were issued for the strictest economy, and when cigarettes were issued after the morning and evening meals, one match only was used to light the entire 21. (There were only five non-smokers).

The menu decided on was as follows:

07.00—One biscuit covered with corned beef, followed by a cigarette.

Noon—Two spoonfuls of condensed milk and one full dipper of water (quarter-pint).

17.30—The same as at 07.00 but with addition of half a dipper of water.

This proved to be an extremely economical bill of fare as it exactly used a 1 kilo tin of meat each meal. At midday too, the ration of milk emptied a 1 lb tin. The tin was then passed to one of the younger, and more junior members of the crew, to be cleaned out, usually by licking the forefinger, after which its edges were bent down and it served as a drinking mug.

Sunday, May 4.

Course maintained. Estimated speed 2 to 3 knots. It was realised that it would be impossible to make the Cape Verdes as the wind was steadily NE to ENE and Force 2 to 4. The main objective was to make as much easting as possible, in order to get into the convoy tracks near Freetown, and ultimately to reach the African coast, about 900 miles distant, should we not be picked up. As there were no instruments of any sort except the compass, any attempt at navigation, beyond guesswork, was impossible. Nevertheless, it was realised that should we go too far North, which was unlikely, we should land in enemy territory and be interned. On the other hand, should we go too far Southward, which seemed to be the tendency, we should eventually sail into the Gulf of Guinea, which would more than double the distance required to make a landfall. However this was all conjecture, and there was very little question in anyone's mind that a convoy would soon be sighted.

This being a Sunday, a double ration of water was issued at noon, and it was decided that for the next few days the water ration could be increased to two dippers (half pint) per man per day, by the issue of a half dipper at the morning meal.

Monday, May 5.

Maintained course. Usual daily routine. The general attitude of the men seemed optimistic and fairly certain that we should be picked up at any time. The wind dropped almost completely at sunset but anti-Trade winds were seen about 21.00. The lower clouds, cumulus stratus, were moving in a SW direction, and the higher banks, consisting principally of cirrus clouds, in a NE'ly. There were rain clouds to the westward, but a change of wind to the SW seemed to be indicated which, it was hoped, would bring them nearer. In view of this possibility a plan for trapping as much rainwater as possible was drawn up, so that no time should be wasted if the rains came.

The men turned in in the usual manner, laying athwart the boat on the oars, which were spread out evenly in the centre. Those who had overcoats wore them, and with a few exceptions there was one blanket to each two men. The boat cover was also spread as an added protection against the damp atmosphere at night and the early morning dew.

Tuesday, May 6.

At about 08.00 the wind veered to SE x S, so course was altered to E x N (magnetic), allowing two points Westerly error and three points for leeway, to make NNE true. It was a comparatively uneventful day but a deal hotter than those previous. Night fell with a promise of rain. The chief officer obtained an error of the compass by bringing the Pole Star right ahead. This gave an error of almost three points West. The variation was believed to be about 20 deg. West, so the resulting deviation of 14 deg. was assumed to be caused by the proximity of the compass to the after lifting hook of the boat. However the compass was steady and behaving admirably so things were left as they were.

Wednesday, May 7.

All hands on deck at 04.00 to catch rain. The sail was lowered and prepared as had previously been arranged but after a few drops the shower passed overhead so the sail was reset and the boat got under way again.

The wind this morning was light and variable, and several men felt that it would be more satisfactory to be pulling on the oars than laying almost becalmed. The mainsail was lowered and the oars manned, but after half an hour it was found to be too wearying in proportion to the progress made, and the attempt was abandoned.

At 11.00 a bathing parade was organised. Each man was permitted to go over the side for a few minutes, but strict orders were issued not to leave hold of the becket lines. While this was in progress an extra man was posted to keep a lookout for sharks. The effect of this dip was excellent; apart from cooling the body and tending to allay thirst it was very heartening to feel that the boat was actually making way, however little, through the water.

It was a week today that the ship was lost. Everybody was still fairly cheerful about things, and usually somebody would say at daylight, "Thank goodness we are going to be picked up today". There was no despondency and mild wagers were being laid as to the exact day and time when the rescue ship would come along. A prize of ten shillings was offered for the first person to sight a ship, and should she subsequently stop and take us aboard it was to be increased to thirty shillings. The rescue ship was never referred to as such, but as "Our Good Neighbour Ship". This was because a certain American company uses this as their slogan, and an American steamer had been heard transmitting a weather bulletin the day before the ship was lost.

The average temperatures were estimated today to be about 98 deg. Fahrenheit by day, and 65 by night.

Thursday, May 8.

At daybreak the wind backed to the NE again so the SE'ly course was resumed. The weather continued as before, slight sea and low easterly swell.

At the morning meal today the first cask of water was emptied. This meant that 26 men had consumed seven gallons in seven days. There still remained one seven and one ten gallon casks, so at the present, rather liberal rate of consumption, this would have been sufficient for a further seventeen days. Any rain caught would considerably lengthen that period. The question of food had, so far, provoked no anxiety. The meat was being consumed at the rate of two tins a day, but there still remained 36. Biscuits had recently fallen into disfavour as they seemed to be thirst provoking. Some men had been finding the meat indigestable during the last two days, and had been having the alternative of two spoonfuls of milk. To date, only eight of the 72 tins of milk had been used.

At about 21.00 a small squid climbed aboard the boat. It had a flying fish firmly grasped in its tentacles. It was slightly larger than a clenched fist, with a dull red colouring and two small, beady eyes protruding from its head. It was hastily ejected and dropped back into the water.

Friday, May 9.

Wind NE. Force 4. Moderate sea and swell. The boat seemed to be making about three and a half knots and was spraying forward occasionally. In order to get as much speed as possible the bathing parade was cancelled today.

There were a number of cases requiring medical treatment. 6th Engineer Withers' arm was washed and redressed. It was still raw, but quite clean and seemed to be progressing as well as might be expected under the circumstances.

Gunner Holmes complained of a cut in his thumb which was badly swollen. This was the first time this man had reported sick although he suffered this cut in abandoning the ship over a week ago. He said that it had become much worse overnight and, on questioning, admitted that he had been one of the men who had handled that squid yesterday evening. The wound was cleansed and dressed, but it obviously needed better treatment than anyone in the boat was in a position to give it.

In the afternoon there were two more patients. One man complained of feeling faint. Aged 21, he was very slight, and seemed less able to stand the strain than the others. He was given sal volatile, and for the rest of the afternoon, and all night, he dozed fitfully, sometimes striking out at those next to him and all the time moaning quietly or mumbling incoherencies to himself.

The other was simply a case of sunstroke and despondency. He was the first man to, in any way, intimate that he was on the verge of giving up hope of being rescued. In this case sal volatile had less effect that a few well-chosen words, but after the heat of the day had passed he seemed to have less difficulty with his breathing, and eventually slept with a certain amount of ease.

After the evening meal the boat was bailed, and before turning in at 19.00, A.B. Blundell and 2nd Steward Wake requested that they might hold a small prayer service for the benefit of any Roman Catholics that were present. It was thought that it would be invidious to make any distinction as to creed and it was decided that anyone who wished to might join in. This met with unanimous response and Wake led the boat's company in the Lord's Prayer, followed, after a few moments of silent meditation, by an impromptu plea for a speedy rescue, both for us and for the crew of the No. 1 boat, of which we had seen nothing for eight days. All hands then piped down except the officer of the watch and the lookout man.

Saturday, May 10.

At 05.15 everyone was awakened as the chief officer sang out: "Men, a ship. God has answered our prayers".

In the breaking dawn a small dot was seen on the horizon to the Westward and a matter of seconds later a red flare had been ignited and was being waved aloft. It seemed at first that she was heading away and three more flares were burned in quick succession. She was then seen to alter course and steer straight for the boat. The sail was kept up for a few minutes longer for the sake of conspicuousness and a treble ration of water was issued to each man.

The sail was then lowered and neatly stowed, the oars were manned and the men were detailed to attend the boat hook and fenders. The ship approached, and was identified as the Elder Dempster liner *Egba*. She hove to to windward, and the boat was pulled over to her as she lowered guess warps and ladders. The men were in fine trim, and pulled on the oars with surprising strength. Once alongside, the boat was evacuated in an orderly manner. It was remarkable that with the exception of the 6th engineer, everyone was able to climb the pilot ladders without assistance. When aboard, the general physical weakness soon became apparent, and it was found almost impossible to remain standing, as the decks of the ship seemed to be lurching in every direction in a particularly violent fashion. Actually, she was lying in a flat calm with practically no movement at all, and our legs, which had been automatically counteracting the short, sharp motion of the boat for nine and a half days, were now creating a movement which did not really exist.

Egba hoisted the boat aboard her after deck and got under way. Mr. Underhill reported to the master, Captain G. D. Simpson, OBE., and supplied him with information necessary for his log book.

CONCLUSION

The position in which the boat was picked up by the *Egba* was latitude 10.57′ North, longitude 29.13′ West. Thus, our course and distance made good was S x W 120 miles. Our rough estimate had been SE 500 miles. This westerly set can only be explained as being due to the North East Trade Drift.

On being torpedoed we were 960 miles from Freetown, and 250 miles from Brava, the nearest of the Cape Verdes. Owing to the drift we had not diminished either of these distances, and that we were picked up at all, in that position, was plainly an act of Providence.

At 15.00 the same day, in position, latitude 11.11′ North, longitude 27.53′ West, the *Egba* sighted a second lifeboat. She closed it, and it was recognised as *Lassell's* No. 1 boat. It was empty, but bore signs of having recently been occupied. The mast had been unstepped and was lying on the thwarts. Several blankets hung over the side, apparently having been used as fenders. The portable radio transmitter was not in the boat, and there was very little water in the bottom. Everything seemed to indicate that her crew had been picked up not many hours previously.

The *Egba* did not pick it up, but continued her voyage to Freetown, where she arrived on the morning of Thursday, May 15.

During these five days, her officers and men did everything in their power to make us comfortable, frequently putting themselves to considerable inconvenience. Mr. Morris, the chief steward, was tireless in his capacity of doctor, dressing and attending the 6th engineer's arm and Gunner Holmes' hand at frequent intervals. It was his opinion that another two days without proper treatment would have seen the onset of serious complications in both cases.

No praise can be too high for the *Egba* ship's company and the entire boat's crew would like to have their very sincere gratitude recorded here.

On arrival at Freetown, a naval launch was sent out, and the chief officer, 6th engineer and 3rd radio officer were taken ashore to the flagship to make a report, while the 3rd officer, with Mr. Swannel of Elder Dempster Lines Ltd., arranged for the men to be accommodated at various hotels.

The eight DEMS ratings came under naval and military control and left the party.

It was arranged that an advance on wages should be issued to enable the men to purchase clothes and toilet necessities, as the naval authorities found themselves unable to do anything in this respect. The difficulty encountered here was that, apart from tropical kit, no clothes were obtainable in Freetown.

During our stay here, Mr. Wheeler, Elder Dempster's general manager, and Mr. Swannel did a great deal of organising on our behalf and secured the best accommodation available. Other ship survivors, who had different agencies, were considerably less well off than ourselves.

Two of the men, A.B. Quinn and O.S. Leicester, agreed to join a British merchant ship, the *Dahomian*, as AB's and commenced duty the following morning. This further reduction brought our party to sixteen, and that afternoon, Friday, May 16, we reported to the naval authorities and were conveyed to the New Zealand Shipping Company's liner *Ruahane* which sailed in convoy the next day, with a passenger list including 81 shipwrecked officers and men.

In conclusion, it seems appropriate to add, that the lifeboat, which was a standard 26-footer, built in 1921, was in every respect highly satisfactory, and made surprisingly little water. With the exception of the top gudgeon, which was pulled off the stern post, there was no untoward incident at all. The equipment was in good condition, especially the compass, which remained steady and easy to steer by throughout the voyage.

There were ample provisions. On being picked up there remained about 14 gallons of water, and milk and meat sufficient for a further seventeen days. The nutritive value of the milk cannot be over-stressed. The meat, which for the first few days afforded a satisfying meal, had later tended to become indigestible.

The first aid equipment was satisfactory, aspirin and sal volatile being particularly useful.

(Signed)
H. W. Underhill, Chief Officer
D. Enticknap, 3rd Officer
May 27, 1941
Aboard *Ruahane*.

The occupants of No. 1 boat were rescued by the Ben Line steamer *Benvrackie* after nine days at sea, but were to face further hardships, for after four days the *Benvrackie* herself was torpedoed and sunk by the submarine *U105*. Fifteen of the original twenty-five who had been taken aboard the *Benvrackie* were lost at this time. The remaining ten, who included Captain Bibby, together with survivors from the Ben liner's crew, were to remain in an open boat for a further thirteen days, during which time a number of men died (none being from the *Lassell's* crew), before being picked up by a hospital ship and landed at Sierra Leone. It says much for their courage that they should survive this second ordeal.

Mr. Underhill after a period at home on leave was promoted master for his next voyage, taking over command of the steamer *Sheridan*. It will be noted that an ordinary seaman, who was amongst the occupants of the No. 2 lifeboat was called D. Leicester, and it is of interest that Mr. Underhill, while serving as second officer of the *Romney* in 1923 served under the command of his father. O.S. Leicester served with Lamport and Holt for many years, and himself rose to the rank of Captain with the company.

Incidentally, Captain Bibby had a brother-in-law who was also a master with the company, Captain W. Watson, and they each had a brother who served as chief officer with Lamport and Holt.

The *Phidias* was the next loss, under the command of Captain E. Parks. She was intercepted by the German submarine *U46* in the North Atlantic on June 8, 1941, which opened fire on the surface, and after a chase she discharged a torpedo which sank the *Phidias*, with the loss of eight of her crew of fifty-one.

The *Balzac* was the next of the fleet to be lost to the enemy, on June 22, 1941, and the following extract is taken from *The Secret Raiders* by David Woodward. (William Kimber, 1955).

On June 22, 1941, a ship was sighted from the German raider *Atlantis* at dawn. As the light improved she was seen to be a medium-sized armed vessel, towards which the *Atlantis* steered a collision course. Rogge (master of the *Atlantis*) opened fire at about 9,000 yards, and the enemy made RRR with her radio, which the *Atlantis* successfully jammed.

Then the British ship began zig-zagging and, handled very skilfully, presented the smallest possible target to her enemy. After forty salvoes—190 rounds—had been fired by the Germans, only four hits had been made, and the forward 5.9 in. battery as well as the No. 5 gun broke down, owing to a defect in the recoil mechanisms. The guns were cooled with sea water and partly manhandled into position. While Rogge turned to bring the disengaged battery, on the other side of his ship, into action. As this was being done the enemy stopped and lowered her boats. She was the *Balzac* of 5,372 tons, from Rangoon to Liverpool with 4,200 tons of rice. Of her crew of forty-seven, four were killed.

In the long running fight the *Balzac* had had plenty of time to have got her RRR through and it was accordingly necessary for the *Atlantis* to disappear from the West side of the South Atlantic.

The *Balzac* was sunk, and the forty-three survivors were taken prisoner, and eventually arrived in Germany where they were to remain for the rest of the war. It had been a gallant effort by the *Balzac* to escape from the raider, but owing to her slow speed it was impossible, but she had still forced the raider to use valuable ammunition, and caused her to change her area of patrol.

The *Biela* under the command of Captain D. Anderson, left Liverpool on January 31, 1942, for Buenos Aires. On February 14, the steamer *Start Point* picked up a distress call indicating that the *Biela* was being attacked by a submarine about 400 miles South West of Cape Race. Nothing was ever heard of the *Biela* or her crew of forty-nine, and it was assumed that she had succumbed to a submarine attack. After the war it was confirmed by German sources that she had been sunk by the submarine *U98*.

The *Willimantic*, a steamer built in the United States in the First World War, was managed by Lamport and Holt, on behalf of the Ministry of War Transport. She was on passage Capetown for Charleston, USA., under the command of Captain Everett, when she was attacked by the submarine *U156*. At the time her chief officer was M. Delaney, and second officer—B. M. Metcalf. The following is the latter's account of the loss.

On June 24, 1942, at 0345 hours we were suddenly attacked by a submarine in position 26N 54W, which opened fire on the surface. First she blew away the wireless room and after end of the chartroom, killing the two radio officers. The next shot blew away the 3.5 in. gun on the poop. I was officer on watch at this time, and the captain tried to keep the submarine astern, but this was difficult because the submarine could not be seen in the darkness, except when she fired her armament. Eventually the ship caught fire amidships, and with shrapnel flying about Captain Everett ordered abandon ship.

The two starboard boats were launched successfully, but the other two were never launched, as a hit was recorded on them whilst they

72

were attempting to put them in the water, killing the third officer, M. Hartley, and an AB; another AB being wounded in the ear.

Captain Everett was taken prisoner on the submarine, and the submarine commander then furnished me with a chart, and having apologised for the sinking of our ship and the deaths of our shipmates, the submarine set off on a North Easterly course, evidently having been on patrol for some time, and being out of torpedoes.

After spreading the boat cover as an awning and rigging up another jury sail, I discussed with the chief officer in the other boat as to his intentions. He decided to steer due West and make for the American coast. I had already decided to make for Antigua, SSW 800 miles, as I thought trying to cross the Gulf Stream was impractical. Mine had the advantage of fair winds and current and estimated I would make it in ten days. He also was of the opinion that they had a better chance of being picked up. I didn't, knowing that in war time ships were routed well away from shipping lanes. After a short discussion I set course SSW and he to the West, but after a while he altered course to the South. We waited until nightfall for him to catch up as he was a few miles behind. (The chief officer's boat landed at St. Kitts, British West Indies, twelve days later.)

When darkness fell I decided to carry on. My next day's noon position showed that we were making three knots, and were still on course. We steered by compass during the day and the stars by night. The sail was a dipping lug only, but we fitted an extra jury sail which helped a lot. The wounded AB was attended to, having a piece of shrapnel in his left ear; this was subsequently removed a fortnight later in hospital at Rio de Janeiro.

During the boat passage I rationed the men to one-eighth of a pint of water daily and one meal consisting of corned beef mixed with crushed biscuit, all we had. During the day the men were kept under cover as much as possible, and wet themselves frequently with sea water, in an effort to keep cool.

On the sixth day in the boat, at about 1000 hours we sighted a ship, and having set off flares, noted that the ship was signalling by Aldis—"Proceeding to pick you up", and altered course towards us. The sail was then taken down, and we went alongside in a seamanlike manner, where having boarded, discovered that she was the Norwegian *Tamerlane*, and at first found my legs to be terribly weak after the boat passage. I was greeted by a stewardess who hugged me, and was weeping profusely. Having reported to the master, Captain Kraft, I informed him as to the other boat, which I estimated to be twenty miles or so to the NNE; he agreed to alter course to search for it, but after a while received a message to the effect that there were submarines in the vicinity, he had to abandon the search.

After seven days they were landed at Rio de Janeiro, and subsequently came home aboard the Royal Mail liner *Highland Monarch*.

The next loss was the *Bruyere* on September 23, 1942, when homeward bound from Buenos Aires. she was torpedoed and sunk by *U125* in the approaches to Freetown, fortunately without loss of life. The crew landed at Freetown in the ship's boats. The following day, the *Defoe* which was only two years old caught fire after an explosion had occurred aboard, which was not directly due to enemy action, the bow being blown off up to the foremast. She was abandoned, and sank shortly after. At the time she had been on a voyage from Manchester to Famagusta with drums of liquid chlorine and aeroplane varnish.

The following month the *Laplace* was torpedoed and sunk by the submarine *U159* on October 29, off the South East African coast, while homeward bound from India. The entire crew survived.

The *Browning* was the next vessel of the fleet to be lost. The following account is by Captain B. M. Metcalf.

The *Browning* under the command of Captain I. Sweeney, sailed from Liverpool, light ship for Barrow, in the early hours of October 1, 1942, following extensive repairs in consequence of grounding along with four or five other vessels in convoy, at Belfast Lough a few months earlier.

At Barrow, she loaded a full military cargo, consisting mainly of ammunition (high explosive shells), tanks, four bulldozers on deck, a large quantity of cased petrol and oil in No. 1 lower hold, and about 100 tons of gelignite and shell fuses in No. 1 'tween deck. Her ballast tanks were thoroughly cleansed and treated, then filled with fresh water.

She eventually sailed from Barrow under sealed orders towards the end of October, joining up with the Liverpool section of a convoy at Liverpool Bay, and later with the Scottish section off Northern Ireland. Altogether there were between fifty and sixty ships. Captain Sweeney of the *Browning* being the Vice-Commodore.

On clearing Northern Ireland, evasive and zig-zag SSW'ly courses were steered under a normal naval escort. The weather being reasonable, a good tight formation was kept, no enemy being sighted, although some occasional depth charging was carried out by the escort, reminding all to be on the alert.

One incident occurred when the chief engineer reported a fracture of about 18 inches in the main intake pipe adjacent to the sea valve, which could be aggravated and prove disastrous in the event of heavy weather and/or extensive depth charging. I was ordered to see if anything could be done, and reported my findings. Whereupon I was told to carry on, and with the assistance of the bosun, carpenter and lamp trimmer, the fractured part of the pipe was paralleled round with burlap strips with a mixture of Stockholm tar and red lead powder, then served tightly round with a one inch wire, and the whole thing was covered with a cement box.

Being under sealed orders, conjecture as to our destination was rife. Some large operation was obvious, rumours spreading thick and fast, and the galley wireless had a rare old time. The captain and I thought North Africa, but when we passed Gibraltar, well to the westward, we gave up surmising. We had steamed about 300 miles southward of the Straits, when we received an Admiralty message to open sealed orders, and learned that the Allied Command were to land at several points on the North African coast. Our destination, the first, being Oran. The message ended to the effect, that this was the start of the Allied offensive and hopefully the turning point of the war, and a large measure of its success depended on the Merchant Service, in whom the command had the utmost confidence.

When darkness fell that night, the convoy turned and headed for a point West of the Straits, which was reached the following night at about 2200 hours. A course was then set East, and the convoy formed into double lines ahead; which must have stretched for at least ten miles. We passed Gibraltar like ghost ships at about midnight and by dawn were all well into the Mediterranean. Apart from an enemy aircraft, nothing else was sighted to give concern; nevertheless all were on the alert and the guns were continuously manned.

At 0800 hours on November 11, the convoy being then 60 miles North of Oran, Captain Sweeney was ordered along with the rest of the Oran section to detach from the main convoy and to commodore the section into Oran. Shortly after, we passed close by the well known passenger ship *Viceroy of India* just as she sank after being torpedoed earlier.

Later a destroyer hailed the *Browning* with instructions to proceed into Arzew Bay, as evidently Oran was not yet clear, the French having put up a lot of resistance. The section anchored in the afternoon, and the *Browning* was boarded by a naval officer, who instructed Captain Sweeney to commodore five other ships into Oran the following day.

The six ships weighed anchor at 1100 hours on November 12, and proceeded double line ahead towards Oran. After rounding the point, course was set South for Oran. Shortly after noon we received orders from the escort to form single line ahead; this was in order to narrow the sweep of the minesweeper ahead, as we were approaching the 100-fathom line.

We were about 12 miles from Oran, when at about 1300 hours there was a violent explosion forward, and the *Browning* shuddered violently, a sheet of flame shot up skywards, and peering through the pall of heavy smoke I could see that the foredeck was aflame, the fore topmast was hanging like a donkey's hind leg, the lower mast leaning at a crazy angle to which was attached the 50-ton heavy lift derrick; one bulldozer had gone over the side to port, and the one on the starboard side was hanging over the side by its lashings which had either stretched or carried away. The fore end of the wheel house was blown in against the steering wheel, the helmsman, fortunately, unhurt, was still standing at his post.

The *Browning* was settling fast by the head, and the order was given to abandon ship, whereupon we launched the lifeboats, and in an effort to clear the ship, with the danger of her cargo exploding, we double banked oars. Later being picked up by a corvette, we had left the *Browning* about twenty minutes, when she being well down by the head, there was a heavy explosion, probably from No. 2 hold, but still the old ship stood firm, then followed another, possibly from No. 4 or 5 hold, and finally a third explosion followed after about five minutes by the grandfather of them all, shooting flame and a pall of smoke which ended in a huge ring miles up in the air. The *Browning* had vanished, literally blown to pieces, parts of which were noted falling into the sea over a wide area.

On making a roll call it was learned that a young deck boy was missing; he had been by No. 1 hatch, when the ship had been hit by the torpedo, and had been blown clean over the side.

Eventually being landed at Oran, we subsequently came home aboard the liner *Empress of Scotland*.

Two days after the loss of the *Browning*, the *Lalande* was hit and damaged by the submarine *U73* in position 36.08′N, 03.46′W, but survived and made port. On June 18, 1943 the *Lalande* was again damaged, this time by an aircraft bomb off Cape Espichel, Portugal, but again she was fortunate in making port.

The Delius homeward bound from India, was attacked by a glider bomb on November 21, 1943, and was badly damaged. As a result she dropped astern of the convoy, and after great efforts by the crew to control the fire aboard, she managed to rejoin the convoy, and subsequently made port. The attack occurred in position 46.46′N, 18.30′W. The following account was compiled by the ship's carpenter.

Just before dawn on a Friday morning, we left a West of England port, bound for India, in convoy, and on our first Sunday at sea a man was lost overboard. Nobody saw him fall, and it was not until the ship astern put up the signal 'man overboard' that it was noticed that he was missing. Each ship in line threw life belts to him as they passed, but by the time the escort reached the spot, he had disappeared.

From that time onwards it seemed as though we had a hoodoo on board; nothing seemed to go right, even the food went bad as the refrigeration went wrong; however nothing else happened until we got into the Indian Ocean. It was at the end of the monsoon season and the weather was very hot when the chief steward was taken ill; after three days of lingering with this illness, which we took to be simply the effects of the heat, he appeared on deck at about 5 o'clock in the morning, lay down in a hammock that was stretched on the boat deck, and died. We were all shocked at this, and began to think that it really was an unlucky trip. We buried him at sea, and those readers who have seen a burial at sea, will agree with me when I say, that it was a very solemn occasion. We carried on from there to our port of discharge in India, and there our bad luck showed itself again.

All hands on board, with very few exceptions, fell ill with malaria or dysentery, or both. We managed to get over it however, and started for home again, wondering what else was in store for us. We were not left waiting long, because we had hardly arrived at the Suez Canal when the chief officer fell ill, and took to his bunk. On arrival at Port Said he was so bad it was decided to put him ashore to hospital. Little did we know that we would not see him again, for four hours after being admitted to hospital he died.

So we left Egypt minus three of our original crew, and fully convinced that fate was not on our side. We safely passed through the Mediterranean and out into the Atlantic Ocean. We had barely got clear of Gibraltar however, when a single enemy plane came out, and commenced to circle the convoy. Keeping well out of range of our guns. Each night he would go away; but the following morning he was back. The fact that he did not attack us convinced us that he was only acting as a spotter for other planes or submarines. After some days like this, it was noted on one day that the 'plane was not to be seen. So we decided that this was the day for our final piece of bad luck.

Sure enough at about 3.15 pm the aircraft warnings sounded and we all took up our stations. Being the ship's carpenter, I was in the repair party, and so I took up my station with the bosun on the boat deck. About nine 'planes came out and most of these got through to the convoy. They first attacked a ship that had dropped astern of the convoy a short distance, owing to some engine trouble; they dropped about ten bombs, of which only one scored a hit, but unfortunately that one was enough to sink her.

After this the *Delius* became the target, and as a bomber came towards us from the direction of the stern quarter, a strange thing happened. A small plane appeared to drop from the rear of the bomber, and gathering speed all the time, flew over the top of the bombers, circled and came at us. We were taken completely by surprise, and thought it was an RAF fighter that had come to protect us. However, as it appeared to be making straight for us, we decided to take no chances, and our gunners fired at it, and scoring a direct hit, it exploded near the ship.

Then it dawned on us that this was Jerry's secret weapon, that we had heard rumours about, and was called a "shelic bomb". The advantage of this new bomb for the enemy, is that the parent 'plane can keep out of range of our guns, and direct his shelic bomb by radio control to whichever target he wishes. This he did to us, after we exploded the first bomb. He flew past and went towards another ship, launched his bomb, which turned around and came back at us.

As I said earlier, I was on the boat deck with the bosun, and with us was an ordinary seaman, and behind us was a gunner. As I saw the bomb coming I shouted to the others to take cover, and dived for a door leading into the funnel, which was the nearest cover available. I had hardly got there with these two seamen when the bomb landed on the foredeck.

I could not move forward or back, but just stood swaying from side to side; the blast hit us from one side then the other, and we saw all kinds of sparks, lumps of wood, metal, and a thick cloud of smoke go past us on the deck. I could not quite realise that we had been hit until I saw that the bosun was badly wounded, and the gunner was staggering around holding his stomach.

The bosun died while I was with him, and after seeing the gunner was being cared for by the first aid party, I went to the foredeck where the lamp trimmer was trying to put out the fire caused by the bomb when it struck No. 3 hold. He was throwing burning bags and pieces of tarpaulin over the side, and after a few minutes we thought that everything was out. Then we saw smoke coming from another hole and we went to investigate, having been joined by other men by this time.

We discovered that it was just smoke coming along the top of the cargo in the shelter deck, so we commenced to cover up again. As we were doing so Jerry came back again and we all tried to find some hole to crawl into for protection, but he was only taking photographs of his handiwork, so we were all right.

We got back amidships to find that besides the bosun, our captain, a steward and an AB had been killed, while quite a number of others were injured.

We sent out a call for a doctor, and shortly afterwards one was transferred aboard. I would like to say here how very good and sympathetic the naval escorts were to us. Every so often a corvette would come as close as possible and ask us if there was anything we needed, and they supplied us with hoses, medical stores, and even cigarettes.

That night we discovered that a piece of hot shrapnel had gone down a ventilator to the lower hold and the cotton which was stowed there was on fire. So a few of us stood by all night, pumping water down the ventilator in a vain effort to extinguish the fire. Next morning came the job of burying our dead. I mentioned before how solemn it is to witness a burial at sea. Imagine it as we watched four of our shipmates, one after the other, go into the sea; men who just a few hours earlier had been very much alive.

Later we took on board three officers from the ship that had been sunk previously; they had volunteered to come on board to help us when they heard that we had only one officer left. And were they a help to us? Right here, I thank God for men like them, who, although they themselves had lost everything when their own ship was sunk, volunteered to go to the help of other comrades who needed help. They cheered us up with their wisecracks and jokes, and at that time we needed their support, because besides the fire we discovered that the water we were pumping into the hold was lodging on the starboard side of the ship and was giving the ship a very bad list.

To make matters worse, a heavy sea came up which held the ship further over. It was so bad that none of us on board thought that she would right herself each time she rolled over. We were expecting her to turn right over, and had that happened not one of us would have been saved. The water in the hold had now penetrated into the steward's stores, entry into which was possible from the main deck.

So we started the portable pumps going to try and pump the water away and to right the ship. The trouble was that the cargo of peanuts in the hold was floating round in the stores and kept getting into the sucker of the pump, stopping the water from going out. As a result at least one of us had to stay down there all the time to keep the suction clear. Some of us were down there at least eight hours at a time. So we carried on for the rest of the voyage, 1,000 miles to go, and the ship on fire with a very serious list to starboard, and with injured men on board.

At times the ship fell back from the convoy, but eventually managed to catch up and keep her station. The engineers, in an effort to save her, drilled holes in the bulkhead between the engine room and No. 3 hold, through which they pumped steam to help control the fire.

In spite of all this we managed to get the ship into a British port. We had no compasses, no degaussing gear, the steering gear was faulty and two of the six cylinders of the engine were out of action. The ship was steered by the stars at night while making port.

I would like to point out that the bringing home of this ship from the point where we were bombed was entirely due to the 28 year old second mate, who was the only officer we had left. On the death of the chief officer he took over the job; and when the captain died he took over the captain's position in command. It was owing to his endurance and good spirits that we were able to carry on.

To give an example, owing to the fact that the dining saloon was wrecked the officers and engineers had to take their meals in the P.O.'s mess, and the table was only meant for six men. Imagine the sight of eighteen men eating in there. It was a common sight to see the officer in command of the ship, sitting on the deck with his plate on his knees, while apprentices and junior engineers were sitting at the table.

We moored at the salvage berth and the Salvage and National Fire Service personnel came on board to take over the job from us. It was a relief to us because for the whole five and a half days we were trying to control the fire, some of us had had no more than five hours sleep per day. We were much amused when the NFS sealed up the stores where we had spent so many hours because, they said, there was a danger of fumes from the peanuts going bad.

Our injured went to hospital, together with men suffering from shock. Two men died in hospital from their injuries, making a total loss of personnel of nine men, including the three prior to the bombing attack.

Our three friends, the officers from the ship that had sunk, left for their homes and sent us a telegram with best wishes, adding, "never were so many peanuts eaten by so few". It took over a week to get the fire aboard the ship under control and it was ten days before we finally docked at Glasgow.

As a result of this ordeal, and for their actions in bringing the *Delius* home, a number of the crew were decorated and commended. A list of such decorations appears elsewhere in these pages.

The last war loss suffered by the company was the *Devis* on July 5, 1943, when she was the commodore ship of a convoy taking part in the invasion of Sicily. She was torpedoed and sunk by the German submarine *U593* in position 37.01′N, 04.10′E. Although none of the crew were lost, she was carrying a large number of troops and there were heavy casualties amongst them. Her valuable cargo of tanks and other equipment was a loss in the subsequent action to take Sicily.

On March 6, 1945 the *Empire Geraint*, managed by Lamport and Holt Line on behalf of the Ministry of War Transport, and under the command of Captain A. R. Bibby, was torpedoed off Milford Haven, by the submarine *U775*, but was subsequently towed into port, repaired, eventually joining the fleet as the *Millais*, the same year.

After the fall of Poland three Polish passenger liners were placed under the management of the company by the Ministry of War Transport and became troopships, running principally to the Far East and India. These were the *Pulaski* of 1912, *Kosciuszko* of 1915 and the 14,287 ton *Batory* of 1936, which was a fast modern liner. All three kept their Polish crews throughout the war, but carried a Lamport and Holt master as liaison officer. At the conclusion of hostilities the *Batory* was handed back to Poland but the crews of the other two ships refused to be repatriated and the vessels were placed under the British flag and their crews signed British articles. They became the *Empire Penryn* and *Empire Helford* respectively and remained under the company's management until they were eventually sold for demolition. Similar arrangements were in being in respect of a number of other vessels of various nationalities. Two Belgian ships, which were taken over by the Ministry at the end of hostilities as troopships, becoming the *Empire Bure* and *Empire Test*, were also managed for a similar period.

During the entire period of hostilities Lamport and Holt were the Liverpool agents for the United States Maritime Commission and handled all their ships using the port.

A number of other ships were managed during the war, including the *Empire Ibex* of 1918, *Empire Franklyn* of 1941, *Empire Dynasty* of 1944, *Samana*, *Samariz*, *Samarovsk* and *Samur*, all of 1943, *Empire Bardolph* of 1943 and *Empire Geraint* of 1942. Of these the *Empire Geraint*, *Empire Bardolph* and *Samariz* were to be purchased under the ship disposal scheme of the British Government, becoming the *Millais*, *Memling* and *Lassell*.

Harland and Wolff Ltd., Belfast delivered two replacement 'D' class ships for those lost; they were the *Devis* in 1944 and *Defoe* in 1945, both taking the names of the ships they replaced.

The service between New York, Brazil and the River Plate was, during the war years, maintained entirely by chartered neutral tonnage.

The *Empire Ibex* was lost as the result of a collision with an aircraft carrier on July 1, 1943. The ship at first remained afloat, but had to be abandoned on July 2 and finally sank a day later, in position 53.36'N, 36.16'W, while under the command of Captain Sweeney, who was in no way responsible for the loss.

A number of other actions took place involving Lamport and Holt ships which are worthy of note. The *Sheridan* had a number of narrow misses during the war; on one occasion in the North Sea a German 'plane dropped a bomb so close that it caused a leak in one of the double bottom tanks. The ship carried on but was eventually drydocked for repairs at Montevideo. On another occasion, while in a homeward bound convoy from Freetown, a submarine surfaced nearby at night and fired a torpedo at the *Sheridan* which took avoiding action; the torpedo missed her but unfortunately claimed another ship in the convoy as victim. The *Sheridan*, being somewhat slow, on more than one occasion fell back, being unable to keep up with a convoy, but survived the war in spite of this.

The following report was made to the naval authorities at Bone, in respect of the success of the *Delane's* A.A. barrage while lying at that port between December 12-17, 1942.

Under continuous air attacks every night while the *Delane* was alongside the wharf at Bone, it can definitely be stated that the security of the ship was dependent on the immediate readiness for use of all the machine guns attached to the vessel, namely four Oerlikons, two Marlins and two Hotchkiss. The way these were manned by the naval and military personnel no doubt, together with the barrage set up by the other vessels in port, protected the number of British merchant ships from being damaged by enemy aircraft.

On Saturday night and Sunday morning of December 12-13 respectively eight enemy 'planes were estimated to have been over the port, five of which were destroyed, three only being claimed by the RAF night fighters, full credit being given to the *Delane* for the destruction of the fourth, and part credit for the crashing of the remaining aircraft was also given to the same vessel.

On the night of December 13, when the port was again attacked by enemy aircraft, the ack-ack barrage of the ship was so intense that the only visible 'plane was immediately engaged while making a dive bombing attack on this particular vessel, and the 20 mm. bullets of the Oerlikon gun fitted on the port side of the boat deck were seen to pierce the 'plane, she was unable to recover from the dive and her remnants were observed the following morning on the opposite side of the harbour amongst civilian property. The position of where the plane crashed was in a direct line from the *Delane*, where she was last observed by the gunners.

(Signed) E. Evans—Armament Officer.
G. E. Roberts—Master.

The *Samarovsk* under the command of Captain D. C. Roberts, while taking part in the Normandy landings, and subsequent supply, claimed a direct hit during this period, parts of the offending plane falling on the deck of the vessel.

During 1943, while crossing the North Atlantic Westbound from London (North about) to New York, the *Balfe* encountered bad weather and, being in ballast, a jury staysail was rigged to help the ship steer; an unusual occurrence for a steamer of this period.

During the period of hostilities a large number of loyal men died whilst serving aboard the company's ships as a result of enemy action. Fifty of the company's seagoing personnel were decorated or received official commendations in recognition of their efforts, as follows:

Name	Rank	Award
Barton, H.	Chief Officer	MBE
Beattie, J.	Chief Engineer	Commended
Bell, R. C.	Ordinary Seaman	BEM
Bibby, A. R.	Captain	OBE
Brazill, L.	Radio Officer	Commended
Byrne, G. F.	Captain	OBE
Conlan, R. J.	Boatswain	BEM
Crapper, E. G.	Second Engineer	Commended
Crowe, J. S.	Second Officer	Commended
Davies, V.	Chief Steward	BEM
Denson, W.	Captain	OBE
Edwards, E.	Boatswain	BEM
Filshie, G.	Chief Engineer	OBE
Geddes, A.	Fourth Engineer	Commended
George, J. H.	Captain	OBE
Gill, J.	Boatswain	BEM
Griffiths, F. A.	Chief Officer	Commended
Hughes, A.	Captain	Commended
Jermyn, E. L.	Chief Officer	MBE
Johnstone, J.	Junior Engineer	Commended
Jones, M.	Chief Steward	BEM
Large, F. W.	Ordinary Seaman	Commended
Little J. A.	Captain	OBE
Loynds, D.	Fifth Engineer	Commended
MacKellar, A.	Captain	Commended
Major, T.	Captain	Commended

Name	Rank	Award
Marshall, G.	Chief Officer	OBE
McPherson, D.	Third Officer	Commended
Merrett, G. C.	Cook	BEM
Metcalf, B.	Chief Officer	Commended
Nye, K. B. K.	Radio Officer	Commended
Owen, I.	Chief Officer	MBE
Page, F. J.	Able Seaman	BEM
Penhale, J. E.	Cadet	Commended
Philpott, A. R.	Carpenter	BEM
Preston, B.	Deck Boy	Mentioned in Despatches
Purton C. G.	Captain	OBE
Reid, J.	Carpenter	BEM
Roberts, D. C.	Captain	OBE
Roberts, G. E.	Captain	OBE
Roberts, M. C.	Cadet	Commended
Rogers, J. A.	Lamp Trimmer	BEM
Rutherford, W. B.	Chief Engineer	MBE
Scott, G.	Captain	Commended
Teunon, F. G. S.	Chief Engineer	Commended
Toy	Chief Steward	Polish Government Award
Underhill, H. W.	Chief Officer	MBE
Watson, A.	Captain	OBE and Polish Government Award
Wood, R. G.	Boatswain	BEM
Williams, S. M.	Second Officer	Commended

The managing director of the Lamport and Holt Line during this period had designed a lifeboat for use in the company's ships, which was later to be adopted by the Ministry of War Transport and which provided more than the usual amount of shelter to the boat's occupants. The following is an extract from the *Evening Express* for January 27, 1944

LIFE-BOAT FOR 55 SAVED 84.

A "Lowe" ship's life-boat—of the type constructed to carry fifty-five persons and described by Ministry of War Transport shipping experts as the safest in the world—has brought eighty-four men to safety.

Mr. Francis H. Lowe, Managing Director of the Lamport and Holt Line, Liverpool, inventor of the life-boat, told the "Evening Express" today that even with eighty-four men aboard the life-boat was by no means near a sinking condition.

This life-boat, which will soon be part of the equipment of all British and Allied merchant ships, had to be launched against a head sea when a British ship was sunk.

The boat was launched much more easily than was expected in such a sea and then came the problem of taking off the crew, eighty-four in a boat built for fifty-five seemed to be asking even too much of the latest life-boat. But they got in and, although cramped and uncomfortable, their extra weight did not adversely affect the seaworthiness of the life-boat.

Some hours later a British destroyer spotted the boat and took the men aboard.

Mr. Lowe spent three years in experimenting before the first boat was finally ready for Ministry of War Transport tests.

He personally bore all expenses—and today stated that he has given the life-boat's secrets to Britain and her Allies. "I have not taken out any patent rights and do not intend doing so", he said, "When something is produced which will save life at sea I think it should be available to all men".

11. THE IMMEDIATE POST-WAR PERIOD

Towards the end of the Second World War a number of organisations cast their eyes towards Lamport and Holt Line Ltd. as a very desirable and asset-laden company well worth acquiring. In the Spring of 1944 United Molasses had offered up to 23/6 (in cash and shares) for each 6/8 Lamport and Holt share. Following this Blue Star Line Ltd, on behalf of Frederick Leyland and Co. Ltd., offered 25/- per share, which in June 1944 was accepted by over 85% of shareholders, and thus the company thereafter came under the control of the Vestey Group. A new management was formed, only Mr. Lowe of the former directors remaining with the company. He became the first general manager, a post he held until his retirement in 1952, although he continued as a director until his death in 1975.

At the conclusion of the war Lamport and Holt owned nine ships, as follows:

Name	Year Built	Gross Tons
Balfe	1919	5,369
Sheridan (1)	1918	4,665
Lalande (2)	1920	7,453
Leighton	1921	7,412
Delius	1937	7,783
Delane	1938	7,761
Debrett	1940	8,104
Devis (2)	1944	8,187
Defoe (2)	1945	8,462

In addition there were four troopships being managed by the company, together with a number of cargo ships yet to be returned to the Ministry of War Transport.

The first acquisitions after the war were two steamers of 7,000 gross tons from the Ministry of War Transport, the *Empire Bardolph* and *Empire Geraint* which became the *Memling* and *Millais* respectively, both useful ships having a limited amount of refrigerated space. The *Defoe* had been completed with some refrigerated space, and in 1945 two other 'D' class ships, the *Debrett* and *Devis*, were returned to the Belfast yard of their builders, Harland and Wolff Ltd., for part of their cargo space to be converted for the carriage of refrigerated cargo.

The following year two more ships were added to the fleet. One was the large *Empire Haig*, which was renamed *Dryden*; she was a most useful ship of almost 10,000 gross tons. The second vessel acquired was the *Celtic*

Star, the first transfer from Blue Star Line, instances of which were to be commonplace from then onwards. This ship had been the *Empire Galahad*, dating from 1942, and acquired by Blue Star in 1946, and within months passed to Lamport and Holt as their *Murillo*. This same year saw the disposal of the *Leighton* after twenty-five years service. She was sold initially for breaking up, but in the event was scuttled in the North Atlantic with a gas bomb cargo.

A significant event in 1946 occurred when the Vestey Group gained control of the Booth Steamship Co. Ltd., also of Liverpool. Both Booth and Lamport and Holt retained their own offices, staff—both seagoing and shore based—and their own ships.

In 1947 the sale took place of the *Sheridan* of 1918 to the Alexandria Navigation Company, for whom she became the *Star of Cairo*, and in 1950 became the *Ocean Endeavour* under the Pakistan flag. She survived thereafter until broken up in 1963. The name *Sheridan* was not to be left out of the fleet for long, as within months the 3,827 gross ton American built ship *Hickory Glen* was acquired, given the name and placed in the trade from New York to South America, which was still at this time being maintained principally with chartered tonnage.

The "Liberty" ship *John J. McGraw* (ex *Samariz*) was bought in this year, becoming the third ship of the fleet to carry the name *Lassell*. In an effort to reinforce the New York service, two fast 'Victory' ships were bareboat-chartered from the Panama Shipping Company, becoming the *Villar* (ex *El Reno Victory*) and *Vianna* (ex *Atlantic City Victory*), both built in 1945. They were very welcome on the route and were granted "Packet Boat" status at Bueno Aires. However, after two years, they were sold by Panama Shipping, becoming the *Bennekom* of the Dutch K.N.S.M. Company and the *Flandres* of Cie Royal Belge Argentina S.A., respectively.

Between 1947 and 1949 three ships were transferred from the Booth Line fleet, being surplus to requirements on the Amazon service from the United Kingdom, where they had been replaced by new and more suitable tonnage. The *Bernard* was the first to be transferred, in 1947, having been built as the *Empire Voice* in 1940 and acquired by Booth in 1946. She was renamed *Byron* by Lamport and Holt. The following year the Booth Line's *Benedict* built in 1930 was transferred, becoming the *Bronte*; and in 1949 the *Boniface* of 1928 arrived to be renamed *Browning*.

An interesting addition in 1950 was a motorship of 6,334 gross tons which had been built at the German yard of Bremer Vulken, Vegesack in 1935 as the *Dusseldorf* for the Norddeutseuer Lloyd. On Christmas Day, 1939 she was captured off the Chilean Coast by H.M.S. *Despatch*. Placed under the Ministry of War Transport as the *Poland* early the following year, she was renamed shortly after as the *Empire Confidence*. In 1946 she was bareboat-chartered to the Alexandria Navigation Company and given the name *Star of El Nil*. Lamport and Holt renamed her *Spenser* and placed her on the service between New York and the River Plate, via Brazil.

The same year saw the disposal of the *Balfe* after thirty-one year's service in the fleet. She was sold to Ali A. Hoborby, who placed her management in the hands of J. Norris and Company, Liverpool, becoming the *Star of Aden*. She was resold twice in 1955 becoming the *Sydney Breeze* and then the *Golden Beta* registered at Hong Kong. She was eventually delivered to the breakers at Osaka on February 1, 1959 after a useful career of forty years. The *Bronte* after only two years in the fleet was sold and became the *Muzaffer* under the Turkish flag.

On December 29, 1950 the *Lalande* of 1920 after thirty years' service with Lamport and Holt was sold, becoming the *Cristina Maria G* under the Italian flag, two years later passing to Panama as the *Cristina Maria*, and finally arriving at Hamburg on August 8, 1959 for breaking up. Also disposed of was the *Browning* in 1951, after two years' service, going to Panamanian flag interests as the *Sannicola*, and resold later the same year, becoming the Japanese *Mizuho Maru*. She sailed as such until February 28, 1961 when she arrived at Mukaishima to be broken up.

Transferred from the Booth Line during 1950 was the modern steamer *Dunstan*, (2,993 gross tons) dating from 1948 when she was completed by Wm. Pickersgill and Sons Ltd., Sunderland. She became the *Sallust* and was for service mainly on the New York service to South America. Another arrival from Blue Star was the 'Liberty' ship *Pacific Star*, built in 1944 as the *Samnid*. On lease-land to Britain for two years, her management was allocated to Blue Star, who bought her outright in 1946. In the Lamport fleet she became the *Lalande*, third steamer in the fleet to be so named, the previous holder of the name having been disposed of only a matter of months earlier. She too, after a short period, was sold to Italian owners and renamed *Ninfea*. In 1959 she passed to the Chinese as the *Nan Hai 147*, and it is not now known whether she is still afloat.

12. NEW SHIPS JOIN THE FLEET

Following the incorporation of both Lamport and Holt Line and the Booth Steamship Company in the Vestey Group, at the end of the war, a heavy rebuilding programme was commenced in respect of both the Blue Star Line and Booth, and for the next few years as those vessels were completed, all surplus tonnage had either been sold out of the group or transferred to Lamport and Holt, as something of a stop gap for them. However, during 1952, the long awaited new ships for the Lamport and Holt Line began to arrive. During this year a steamer and two motorships were delivered to their order. The *Romney*, a turbine steamer of 8,237 gross tons, built by Cammell Laird and Co. Ltd., Birkenhead, became the company's flagship, a position she was to hold for twenty-six years. A motorship of similar tonnage, the *Raeburn*, was delivered by Harland and Wolff Ltd., Belfast. Both these ships were designed for service between the United Kingdom and Brazil and the River Plate. The other ship was the 4,459 gross tons *Siddons* which came from the Sunderland yard of William Pickersgill and Sons Ltd. for the trade from New York to Brazil and the River Plate.

A further 'Liberty' ship was also transferred from Blue Star Line during this year; she had been built in 1944 as the *Samannan* and managed until 1946 by Blue Star who then bought her outright to become their *Oregon Star*. In the Lamport and Holt fleet she became the *Laplace*. During the year two 'M' class ships were disposed of. The *Millais* (2) being transferred to Blue Star to become their *Oregon Star*, being something of a swap with the vessel of the same name previously described. But it should be noted that the ship transferred from Lamport's to Blue Star had part refrigerated space, whereas that transferred the other way had none. The *Murillo* (2) was sold out of the group, going to the Italian flag as the *Bogliasco*. In 1963 she was renamed *Ocean Peace*, trading under the Panamanian flag, finally arriving at Kaohsiung on September 13, 1967 for breaking up. Also transferred to Blue Star during this year was the *Dryden* (3) which became the *Fremantle Star*, and in 1958 the *Catalina Star*. Five years later she was to return to the Lamport and Holt Line.

A further 'R' class ship, the *Raphael*, was delivered in 1953, designed for the United Kingdom-South American trade. A motorship of 7,971 gross tons, built by Bartram and Sons Ltd, Sunderland, she was the fastest ship launched at that yard up to that date, achieving 17½ knots on her trials. These 'R' class vessels were to be some of the most outstanding, in terms of lines, ever to join the fleet.

Transferred from Blue Star during this year was the *Columbia Star* dating from 1939, which became the *Dryden* (4). Sold to Panamanian flag operators was the 'Liberty' ship *Laplace* (3) after only one year in the fleet. Transferred to Blue Star was the *Memling* (3) which became the *Vancouver Star*, for service on the Blue Star Line trade from Liverpool and Glasgow to the North Pacific coast ports of the United States and Canada, a trade in which a number of Lamport and Holt ships were to be involved, having been bareboat or time-chartered, or transferred to Blue Star for the purpose. This interest greatly increased with the acquisition of the Donaldson Line's share of the trade, and Lamport and Holt were agents for all these ships operating from Liverpool.

During the preceding few years three ships designated as the 'B' class were disposed of and, there being only one left, the *Byron*, she was renamed *Lalande* (4) to bring her into line with other units of the fleet.

The following figures give some idea of the size of the fleet over the years up until 1953.

Year	No. of Ships	Total Gross Tonnage
1875	31	48,236
1888	50	93,331
1890	59	109,493
1894	49	100,731
1914	36	198,992
1924	50	322,857
1936	21	144,062
1939	21	141,003
1945	9	65,396
1953	16	105,970

As can be seen the fleet had made a good recovery by 1953 and was approaching the strength at which it had entered the war in 1939. Another interesting point revealed is that the number of ships owned in 1953 as compared with the 1890s had dropped to less than a third, while the tonnage overall in 60 years had been maintained with the increased size of individual ships.

The year 1953 is a good one to study the breakdown of the fleet into trades and groups of ships. There were still five 'D' class ships, three of which had refrigerated space, and the *Dryden* which was also so equipped; two 'L' class and three modern 'R' class ships, all being general cargo ships. Of these most were engaged on the United Kingdom to Brazil and River Plate trades, although occasionally over the previous few years a 'D' class ship was to be seen in New Zealand, having been time-chartered by the outward conference lines to New Zealand, and loading homewards on Blue Star's berth. On rare occasions an 'R' class ship was to be seen loading at a West Coast of the United States or Canadian port for Liverpool. The four remaining, bore 'S' names, although all were entirely different, trading on the New York service to Brazil and the River Plate.

On December 24, 1953 an interesting event occurred when the motorship *Rampart* (863 gross tons) departed from Liverpool on time-charter to the Lamport and Holt Line. It marked the inauguration of a direct service between the United Kingdom and the Paraguayan port of Asuncion by the company. This voyage, lasting seventy-seven days, was under the command of Captain W. C. Pargeter, of Ary Shipping Ltd., the *Rampart's* owners. Arriving at the Paraguayan capital on January 22, 1954, she was believed to be the first British ship ever to reach the port, no records being in existence of any other visit. After discharging general cargo, mainly consumer goods ranging from cosmetics, shoe polish and spirits, together with machinery and spares for Paraguayan export industries, she loaded tinned meats homewards, leaving Asuncion on January 30. So successful was this venture that more tonnage was chartered and a regular service commenced, subject to the levels of the Rivers Parana and Paraguay, which at that time were most difficult to navigate as there were no lights or buoys marking the channel. Eventually two ships were acquired for this trade.

A further vessel was acquired for the New York service in 1954, when the *Sargent* joined the fleet from Booth, having been on bareboat-charter to them since 1946 from the Panama Shipping Company, having traded as the *Jutahay*. She had been built in 1945 by Walter Butler Shipbuilders Inc., Duluth. Of 3,843 gross tons she was launched as the *Frank J. Petrarca* and completed as the *Roband Hitch*. It is interesting to note that Lamport and Holt registered her at Port of Spain, Trinidad for the eight years that she remained in the fleet.

An interesting transaction took place in this year when the Vestey Group bought the refrigerated ship *Mosdale* (3,022 gross tons) from A/S Mosvold Shipping, Norway. She had traded for them since her completion by Burmeister and Wain, Copenhagen in 1939. At first she was placed under the ownership of Blue Star as *Albion Star*, but this was quickly changed and she became the *Balzac* for the Lamport and Holt Line. She was to trade almost entirely with bananas from Santos to the United Kingdom and Continent, or on time charter to Geest Industries on their run from Dominica to Preston and occasionally to Barry. In 1955 an almost identical vessel built a year earlier at the same yard for Cie. Générale d'Armement Maritime, France, as the *Barfleur*, joined the fleet, becoming the *Boswell*. Both were good looking ships with their white painted hulls and blue boot topping.

Blue Star were rapidly expanding their fleet engaged on the trade from Liverpool and Glasgow to the North Pacific coast ports of North America and during 1954 and 1955 all five 'D' class ships were transferred to them, the *Delius* becoming the *Portland Star*; *Delane*—*Seattle Star*; *Defoe*—*Geelong Star*; *Debrett*—*Washington Star*; and the *Devis*—*Oakland Star*. In 1956 the *Debrett* and *Devis* reverted back to Lamport and Holt and their original names.

During 1955 the service from New York as far South as the River Plate was discontinued, and the remaining ships transferred back to the United Kingdom, or employed from New York to the West Indies, North Brazil and the Amazon. Close ties were established between them and the Booth Line ships so employed, and they began to run in conjunction. At about this time an interest was taken in a service from Montreal to the West Indies and Georgetown. In the event the *Siddons* (3) and *Spenser* (3) were transferred back to the United Kingdom where they were renamed *Rubens* and *Roscoe* respectively, falling in with the 'R' class vessels on this route. These two ships mostly traded to Brazilian ports, their size being particularly useful at small coffee and timber ports.

Although small vessels continued to be chartered for the Asuncion service, two such ships were acquired by the company. The *Verdi* of 571 gross tons in 1955, from a Dutch owner, having been completed as the *Hermes* the previous year; and the *Virgil* in 1956, having been launched as the *Manstead*, she was completed for the Panama Shipping Company and bareboat-chartered by Lamport and Holt. She was the smallest ship in the fleet at 404 gross tons.

In 1956 the *Rossetti*, a sistership of the *Rubens* (ex *Siddons*) was delivered by Wm. Pickersgill and Sons Ltd., Sunderland. She too was to trade mostly to Brazilian ports from the United Kingdom, being a particularly useful ship at shallow draft ports.

A number of ships were transferred from Blue Star in 1957. Having spent four years as the *Vancouver Star* the *Memling* (3) returned and reverted to her former name. In addition two other war built 'Empire' ships were transferred. One, the *Murillo* (3), was built in 1944 by Lithgows Ltd., of Port Glasgow, as the *Empire Talisman* for the Ministry of War Transport, and placed under Blue Star's management. She was bareboat-chartered by them between 1946 and 1949, purchased outright in 1949 and became the *Tacoma Star*. The other ship, built in the same year as the *Murillo* but by Short Bros. Ltd., Sunderland, as the *Empire Pendennis*, was placed under the management of Ellerman's and in 1946 became the *Vasconia* for Cunard, and the *Fresno City* for Blue Star in 1951. She traded as the *Millais* for Lamport and Holt.

A further 'R' class vessel appeared from Bartram and Sons Ltd., Sunderland, in 1957; she was a sister ship of the *Raphael*, and was named *Ronsard*. Initially she was registered at Hamilton, Bermuda in the ownership of Salient Shipping Co. (Bermuda) Ltd., not transferring to the Liverpool register until 1960.

During 1957/58 the *Romney*, under the command of Captain B. M. Metcalf, completed six round voyages between Montreal, the West Indies and Georgetown, where her extra capacity was found to be most useful.

The second ship to bear the name *Sallust* was transferred back to Booth after seven years in the fleet, reverting to her former name of *Dunstan*, and at the same time another ship in the Booth fleet transferred to Lamport and Holt. Amazingly this was another *Dunstan* which had been built in 1945 in the United States, launched as the *Tulare*, and completed as the *Coastal Challenger*. Acquired by the Panama Shipping Company in 1946 she was renamed *Pachitea* on bareboat-charter to Booth, and bought outright by them in 1954 to become the *Dunstan*. She naturally became the new *Sallust* for Lamport's on the New York service.

In 1958 the *Raeburn*, after a mere six years, was transferred to Blue Star Line for service to the North Pacific, becoming their *Colorado Star*. She was a particularly fine vessel, and, as was the case with a number of such transfers, she remained registered at Liverpool under Lamport's ownership until 1972 when Blue Star, having commenced container services on this route, transferred her to the Austasia Line and renamed her *Mahsuri* under the Singapore flag. During the fourteen years trading to the West Coast ports of the United States and Canada, Lamport and Holt Line continued to be her agents and loading brokers at Liverpool, as they were for the rest of the Blue Star fleet at the port.

During 1958 the *Delius* and *Defoe* both reverted back to Lamport and Holt and their original names, but the *Delane* remained with Blue Star as the *Seattle Star* until sold out of the group in 1961. After a delivery voyage as the *Kettara VI*, she arrived at Hong Kong on October 13, 1961 for breaking up. The following year the *Sallust* (3), after only one year on the New York service, was transferred to the Austasia Line. Renamed *Malacca*, she traded as such until 1962 when sold to Kie Hock Shipping Company, of Hong Kong, and having sailed from Kawasaki for Singapore on October 25, 1967 she was lost without trace. The *Memling* (3) arrived at Flushing on October 23, 1959 where she was broken up.

Two small motorships were built in 1959 for the New York service. They were particularly suitable for the Amazon trade since they were able to reach the Peruvian port of Iquitos. They were the *Siddons* of 1,282 gross tons from George Brown Ltd., Greenock, and the similar *Spenser* from Noderwerft Koser and Meyer, Hamburg.

During this year a 3,000 gross ton refrigerated ship was delivered from the yard of Brooke Marine Ltd., Lowestoft. Named *Constable* she was at the time the largest vessel delivered from this yard. A fast ship, with clipper-like lines, she was followed early the following year by a sister, the *Chatham* from A. Stephen and Sons Ltd., Linthouse. Both were used on a variety of trades, and were to be seen trading between Dominica and

93

Preston and Barry on charter to Geest, but also trading to Trinidad, Santos and the East Coast of the United States from Dublin. Their much older consorts, *Balzac* and *Boswell* were renamed *Carroll* and *Crome* to fall into line with this 'C' class, but were quickly transferred to Blue Star, becoming the *Norman Star* and *Roman Star*. In the same year they passed to the Booth Steamship Co. Ltd., as the *Bede* and *Basil*. First to leave the group was the *Bede* in 1963, when she became the Greek *Victoria Elena*, and was subsequently burnt out following a fire in her cargo of cotton on January 16, 1967. Her sister *Basil* was sold in 1964 and after a succession of names and owners (1964 *Eleni K*, 1966 *Eleni Kyriakou*, 1969 *Olga*, 1970 *Georgios Markakis*, 1973 *Nikos*) was finally broken up in 1973, after a useful career of thirty-four years. In that time she had carried no less than eleven names, five while owned within the Vestey Group.

During 1960 the *Sheridan* (2) and *Millais (3)* were disposed of. The *Sheridan* transferred to the Singapore based Austasia Line as the *Matupi*, and was sold in 1964 to the Kie Hock Shipping Company, Hong Kong, becoming the *Tong Lam*. She was resold in 1968 without change of name and again in 1970. On October 27, 1970 she went aground and became a total loss while on passage North Korea to Chittagong. The *Millais* was sold for further trading to the Grosvenor Shipping Co. Ltd., who renamed her *Grosvenor Navigator*. She arrived at Kaohsiung on September 9, 1966 for breaking up. March 16, 1961 saw the arrival of the *Murillo* (3) at Vigo for breaking up, and the *Delius* after a delivery voyage as the *Kettara VII* arrived at Tokyo on February 24, 1962 for breaking up. The *Lalande* after becoming the *Uncle Bart* arrived at Moji for demolition on September 8, 1961.

In 1961, a new motorship named *Sheridan* (3) of 1,535 gross tons, joined the fleet from T. van Duijvendijk's Scheepswerf N.V. Lekkerkerk, for the New York service, while the *Spenser* (4) was transferred to the Booth Line and renamed *Valiente*. The following year saw the arrival of a sister ship from the same yard as the *Sheridan*, which was named *Spenser* (5).

Meanwhile the service to Asuncion direct from the United Kingdom by the *Verdi* and *Virgil* continued, supplemented as required by the time-chartering of additional tonnage. These small ships usually loaded machinery, general cargo and spirits, at London, Liverpool or Glasgow and made calls outwards and homewards at Dakar and Montevideo for refuelling and stores. They did not always make it as far as Asuncion, depending on the level of the Rivers Panama and Paraguay. Captain F. Martin made three voyages in the *Verdi* during 1961/62 and only on one of these was he able to make it as far as Asuncion. On another voyage he was warned of the situation by the master of the chartered Dutch vessel *Nashira* who, on learning that the chartered *Dita Smits* was stranded further up river, turned back to Santa Fe, where his cargo was discharged for transhipment into even smaller vessels. His example was followed by the *Verdi*. On another occasion the *Verdi* was able to go as far as Pto. Praia, only fifty miles from Asuncion, where she moored to the river bank and discharged into lighters.

During 1962, while homeward bound, the *Virgil* under the command of Captain R. P. Willis broke down, her main thrust bearing having broken beyond repair, and after days drifting helplessly in mid-Atlantic, the *Verdi* (Captain Martin), which was outward bound, was contacted and commenced to tow the *Virgil* at 12.25 hours G.M.T. on April 3, in position 05.13′N, 22.46′W. Two mooring ropes tied end to end were used, paying out a little extra each day to compensate for the strain, and the vessels arrived back at Dakar Roads at 21.15 hours G.M.T. on April 10, where repairs were effected.

During 1962 seven ships were disposed of by Lamport and Holt. The *Devis* (2) after eighteen years afloat, arrived at Spezia on July 4, 1962 where she was broken up. The *Sargent* passed to Greek owners as the *Pamit*, being resold in 1966, and taking the Liberian flag as the *Bambero*. She finally arrived at Castellon for demolition on March 3, 1970. The *Roscoe* was broken up and the *Lassell* was sold for further trading. The other three units passed to Vestey Group companies, the *Chatham* and *Constable* going to Blue Star, who renamed them *Mendoza Star* and *Santos Star* respectively. The *Siddons* (4), only three years old, was bareboat-chartered to Booth under the name *Veras*. This left the two 'S' class ships *Sheridan* and *Spenser* trading from New York in conjunction with the vessels of the Booth Steamship Co. Ltd.

In 1963 the sale of the *Verdi* and *Virgil* took place, both passing to the Dutch flag as the *Kilo* and *Metre*. They were quickly taken on time-charter by Lamport and Holt's wholly owned subsidiary, the Metric Line, trading from Liverpool to Rotterdam. Thereafter the Asuncion service was wholly maintained with chartered vessels. Later in 1963 the *Verdi* put into Swansea Bay in distress, her deck cargo of sodium having started to explode. She was beached and the crew rescued by the Mumbles lifeboat which had considerable difficulty in catching her in the particularly bad weather on that November night. She was subsequently repaired and returned to service.

The other disposal that year was the *Rossetti* (2) which was transferred to Booth and renamed *Boniface* for service between Liverpool, the West Indies and the Amazon. Four ships were to enter the fleet, however. Two medium sized ships, the *Wanstead* and *Woodford* were time-chartered from Watts, Watts and Co. Ltd., being renamed *Raeburn* and *Rossetti* for the duration of the charter. Almost a year later both reverted back to their former names at the conclusion of the charter, and the much larger *Weybridge* was then chartered for a short period during which she was also named *Rossetti*. The other acquisitions were transfers from Blue Star.

The *Catalina Star* (ex *Fremantle Star*) and *Columbia Star* (ex *Patagonia Star*), which had both previously traded for Lamport and Holt as the *Dryden*. The former was renamed *Devis* and the latter reverted to the name *Dryden*.

The *Debrett* was disposed of during 1964, becoming the *Ambasciata*, and arrived at Osaka on December 28 of that year for breaking up. She was followed the next year by the *Rubens* (ex *Siddons*) which passed to Booth Line as the *Bernard* for service to the Amazon from Liverpool. The last of the traditional 'D' class ships, the *Defoe* was sold in 1966. She was renamed *Argolis Star*, trading as such for a further three years before her arrival at Shanghai on October 29, 1969 for breaking up. Her place in the fleet was taken by the *Rubens* (3), which dated from 1951, having been completed as the *Crispin* by Wm. Pickersgill and Sons Ltd., Sunderland. She had passed to the Austasia Line in 1953 as the *Mandowi*, reverting back to Booth earlier in 1966, before transferring to Lamport and Holt.

The year 1967 marked the withdrawal of Lamport and Holt Line tonnage from New York when the two remaining ships, *Sheridan* and *Spenser* were transferred to Booth and renamed *Cyril* and *Cuthbert*. This connection, which had lasted for almost one hundred years, was carried on alone by the Booth Line until 1977, when they withdrew.

Three moderately sized vessels were transferred from Booth in this year. The *Bernard* (ex *Rubens*, ex *Siddons*) which became the *Rossini*, her third name in the Lamport fleet, there already being a *Rubens* in the fleet at this time; the *Boniface* (ex *Rossetti*) which reverted back to her former name; and a ship with an interesting career, which had also been built by Pickersgill's. This vessel, laid down as the *Clement* for Booth, was launched as the *Malay Star* for Blue Star, but was completed in 1953 as the *Malay* for the Austasia Line, for which she became the pioneer vessel. She was renamed *Mahsuri* in 1964, before reverting back to Booth's as the *Benedict*. In the Lamport and Holt fleet she became the *Renoir*. All three were particularly useful on the Brazil service from the United Kingdom. The following year saw the departure of the *Dryden* (4) for breaking up, arriving at Kaohsiung in November, 1968. Her place was taken by the *Dunedin Star* of 1950 from Blue Star, which was renamed *Roland*. During the next three years four ships were disposed of while none were acquired. This was in part due to the expansion of a number of national flag shipping enterprises, and the routing of cargo onto their vessels. The four ships disposed of were: 1969—*Devis* (3), 1970—*Rossini* and *Rossetti*, and 1971—*Renoir*.

In 1972 the Blue Star liner *Canadian Star*, built in 1957, joined the fleet to become the *Raeburn*. During that year she loaded on one occasion on the Blue Star Line berth at Liverpool for South Africa, but the remainder

The "Devis" of 1938 was a war loss in 1943.

(Harland and Wolff Ltd.)

A wartime view of the first "Devis".

(A. Duncan)

The "Defoe" (1) being launched at Harland and Wolff Ltd., Belfast in 1940. She was lost two years later.
(Harland and Wolff Ltd.)

The "Debrett" on trials in 1940.

(Harland and Wolff Ltd.)

The heavily armed "Debrett" during the Second World War.

(A. Duncan)

A post-war view of the "Debrett".

(Skyfotos Ltd.)

The "Devis" (2) of 1944.

(Skyfotos Ltd.)

The "Defoe" (2) of 1945.

The Polish liner "Batory" (14,287 gross tons) of 1936 was managed throughout the war by Lamport and Holt Line.
(Skyfotos Ltd.)

The Polish liner "Kosciuszko" of 1913 was managed by the company during the war. Following hostilities she was renamed "Empire Helford" by the Ministry of War Transport, the company continuing to manage her until the 1950s.

(T. Rayner)

The Troopship "Empire Bure" was managed by Lamport and Holt during the immediate post war period.

(T. Rayner)

The Troopship "Empire Test" managed by the company.

(T. Rayner)

The Troopship "Empire Test".

(T. Rayner)

MEMLING

Built in 1943 as the "Empire Bardolph", the "Memling" (3) was acquired in 1945.

(A. Duncan)

Formerly the "Empire Geraint" of 1942, the "Millais" (2) was purchased in 1945.

(World Ship Photo Library)

The "Dryden" (3) (ex "Empire Haig") served the company as such from 1946 to 1952.

(A. Duncan)

The "Dryden" (3) returned to Lamport and Holt in 1963 but under the name "Devis" (3).

(A. Duncan)

The Liberty ship "Lassell" (3) joined the fleet in 1947.

(Skyfotos Ltd.)

The "Lalande" (4) had previously been named "Byron" (2).

(A. Duncan)

The Victory ship "Vianna" was bareboat-chartered from Panama Shipping Company Inc., in 1947.

(T. Rayner)

Built in 1930 for the Booth Line, the "Bronte" (2) was transferred to Lamport and Holt in 1948.

(A. Duncan)

The "Spenser" (3) was acquired for the New York—Brazil and River Plate service in 1950. German built she had been taken as a war prize by the Royal Navy in 1939.

(A. Duncan)

Transferred from the New York service to the United Kingdom in 1955 the "Spenser" was renamed "Roscoe".

(Skyfotos Ltd.)

The "Sallust" (2) was transferred from the Booth Line in 1951.

(World Ship Photo Library)

Built for the New York, Brazil and River Plate service in 1952, the "Siddons" (3) was a product of Wm. Pickersgill and Sons Ltd., Sunderland.

(World Ship Photo Library)

Transferred to the United Kingdom in 1955, the 'Siddons'' was renamed "Rubens'' (2).

(A. Duncan)

Having spent two years with the Booth Line, The "Rubens" (ex "Siddons") returned to the Lamport and Holt Line in 1967 as the "Rossini".

(A. Duncan)

The turbine steamer "Romney" (2) was built in 1952 by Cammell Laird and Co. Ltd., Birkenhead. She was the company's flagship for over twenty years.

(Skyfotos Ltd.)

The "Romney" (2) had a career of twenty-six years under the Lamport and Holt Line houseflag.

(Skyfotos Ltd.)

The "Raeburn" (2) of 1952 was a product of Harland and Wolff Ltd., Belfast.

(Skyfotos Ltd.)

Having spent nineteen years with Blue Star Line or Austasia Line, the "Raeburn" (2) returned to Lamport and Holt in 1977 as the "Roland" (2). She was broken up in 1978.

(A. Duncan)

Built in 1939 as the "Columbia Star" for the Blue Star Line, the "Dryden" (4) was to spend two periods trading for Lamport and Holt between 1953 and 1968.

(Skyfotos Ltd.)

The "Raphael" (2) was built in 1953 by Bartram and Sons Ltd., Sunderland.

(Skyfotos Ltd.)

A rare view of the "Raphael" at Vancouver in 1959.

(F. W. Hawks)

The "Raphael" (2).

(A. Duncan)

The small motorship "Verdi" (2) was acquired in 1955 for the direct Asuncion Service.

(Capt. F. Martin)

The "Verdi" tied up to the river bank at Pto. Praia in the River Paraguay, just fifty miles from Asuncion.

(Capt. F. Martin)

The small "Virgil" was bareboat-chartered from Panama Shipping Co. Inc., in 1956 for the Asuncion service.
(A. Duncan)

COSCO, China. Renamed **AN FU JIANG.**

...., 9,024/76. by Lamport & Holt Line Ltd. to China Ocean Shipping

1984

J. Prentia

BROWNING 28/3/81

COMTE DE NICE as NAIAS, 18/7/83

L. W. C. Lamers

CAST CORMORANT. (Nordic Clipper—81, Naess Viking—74), 72,728/72—m.obo carrier. Has been renamed PACIFIC JASMIN by Core Combination Carriers Inc. Liberia.

CAST NARWHAL. (Nordic Conqueror—80, Naess Ambassador—74), 132,305/72—s.ore/oil carrier. By Core Combination Carriers Inc. to Calyx Corp. then Ber Ships Inc. all Liberia. Renamed CASTOR.

CAST ANDINO. (Turquoise Beauty—82), 5,306/77—m.ro-ro vessel. Has been renamed CCNI ANTARTICO. (Opal Bounty—82), 5,311/77—m.ro-ro vessel. Has been renamed STRIDER FEARLESS by Strider 5 Ltd., Liberia.

STRIDER EXETER by Strider 4 Ltd., Liberia.

CENTENNIAL LION, (Johnstone Straits—79, James W. Curley—54), 303/44—Wood tug. By W. Church to Krussion Katboats Inc., both Canada. Name unchanged.

CHARLEVOIX. 535/62—m.ferry. By La Compagnie de Navigation Charlevoix-Saguenay &te. to Government of Canada (Ministry of Transport & Communications for the Province of Ontario) both Canada. Name unchanged.

CHESHIRE, 19,061/71—m.bulker. By Britain S.S. Co. Ltd. to Ambersley Ocean S.A., Greece. Renamed MARIA.

CHRISTOS TH, (Myofuku Maru—77), 400/65—Panther Marine Co. Ltd. Name should CLADYKE. (Westondyke—82). 696/71. By Cornish Shipping Ltd. to Naviera Cuyamel S.

CHRISTO TH.

CLAFFEN, R.L., Honduras. Renamed CARMEN

CLAFFEN, (Fendyke—82), 696/71. By Cornish Shipping Ltd. to Naviera Cuyamel S. de R.L., Honduras. Renamed PAQUITA.

CLARENVILLE, 334/44. By Bonaventures Ltd. to Highland Cove Marina Ltd. both

The "Rossetti" (2) of 1956.

(Skyfotos Ltd.)

The "Ronsard" of 1957 was a sistership of the "Raphael".

(Skyfotos Ltd.)

The "Ronsard" was originally registered at Hamilton, Bermuda transferring to the Liverpool Register in 1960.

(A. Duncan)

The "Murillo" (3) was transferred from Blue Star in 1957.

(A. Duncan)

The "Millais" (3) was another transfer from Blue Star in 1957.

(A. Duncan)

The "Siddons" (4) was built in 1959 for the New York/West Indies/Amazon service. She is seen under her later name of "Veras" whilst on bareboat-charter to the Booth Steamship Co. Ltd.

(A. Duncan)

The "Sheridan" (3) was built in 1961 for the New York/West Indies/Amazon service.

(A. Duncan)

The refrigerated ship "Constable" was built in 1959 by Brooke Marine Ltd., Lowestoft.

(Skyfotos Ltd.)

The "Chatham" (2) was a product of A. Stephen and Sons Ltd., on the Clyde.

(Skyfotos Ltd.)

The motorship "Woodford" was chartered from Watts, Watts and Co Ltd., in 1963, and renamed "Rossetti" (3).

(A. Duncan)

The "Wanstead" was chartered in 1963 and renamed "Raeburn".

(A. Duncan)

Having spent fifteen years with Booth Line and Austasia Line, the "Rubens" (3) was transferred to the Lamport and Holt Line in 1966. (Skyfotos Ltd.)

The "Rubens" (3) had been built in 1951.

(A. Duncan)

The "Renoir" was acquired in 1967. She is seen with the Austasia Line funnel colours during a period on charter.
(A. Duncan)

The steamship "Dunedin Star" built in 1950, was transferred in 1968 becoming the "Roland" (1).

(A. Duncan)

Acquired in 1972, the "Raeburn" (4) was originally Blue Star Line's "Canadian Star".

(A. Duncan)

Launched on October 31st, 1978, the SD14 "Bronte" (3) is seen on Trials.

(Turners (Photography) Ltd.)

The "Browning" (3) was one of four SD14 cargo ships built for the Lamport and Holt Line by Austin and Pickersgill Ltd., Sunderland. All were completed in the period 1979/1980.

(A. Duncan)

The "Browning" and her sisterships were equipped to carry 118–20ft containers.

(Skyfotos Ltd.)

The SD14 cargo ship "Boswell" (3) of 1979.

The launch of the "Belloc" at Austin and Pickersgill Ltd., Sunderland, on May 10th, 1979.

(Austin and Pickersgill Ltd.)

The SD14 "Belloc" of 1980.

(Skyfotos Ltd.)

Built in 1979 as the "Ruddbank", the "Romney" (3) was acquired in 1983.

(J. A. MacLeod)

Built in 1979 as the "New Zealand Star", the "Churchill" was lengthened at Singapore in 1986 for the Europe to East Coast of South American Container Service.

(FotoFlite)

The "Churchill", with a capacity of 1,143 containers, is one of nine such ships operating in a Consortium between Europe and the East Coast of South America.

(FotoFlite)

The ''Churchill'' entered Lamport and Holt Line service in April, 1986 when she commenced loading at Montevideo for Europe. She is seen in the English Channel in May, 1986 outward bound for Brazil.

(Fotoflite)

of her service for Lamport and Holt was spent trading from Liverpool, Glasgow and Swansea to Brazil and the River Plate. The following year saw the departure of the *Rubens* (3) for further trading under the Greek flag. Her departure left the five 'R' class ships maintaining the Lamport and Holt services from the United Kingdom.

During 1974 the Vestey Group acquired premises at 30, James Street, Liverpool, from the Pacific Steam Navigation Company. This building was erected in 1892 as Oceanic House and was originally the headquarters of the White Star Line. The building was refurbished and renamed Albion House. This coincided with the formation of a new company, under the title Blue Star Ship Management Ltd., which took over responsibility for the ship husbandry of all the ships owned and/or operated by Lamport and Holt Line Ltd., the Booth Steamship Co. Ltd., and Blue Star Line Ltd. and was originally based at Liverpool, but almost a decade later was to be moved to Albion House, Leadenhall Street, London. During the earlier part of 1975 the managements of both Lamport and Holt and Booth Line moved to the new building at Albion House, Liverpool, thus the connection between Lamport and Holt and the Royal Liver Building, which had been its headquarters since 1912, came to an end.

During 1975 the *Roland* (1) was disposed of, followed a year later by the *Raphael* (2). In January 1977 the *Mahsuri*, which had originally been the *Raeburn* from 1952 to 1958, returned to the Lamport and Holt Line to be renamed *Roland* (2). Thus the fleet consisted of four 'R' class vessels as follows:- *Romney* (2) of 1952, *Roland* (2) of 1952, *Ronsard* of 1957 and the *Raeburn* (4) of 1957.

13. CONTAINERISATION

There has been a dramatic change in South America's trade with Europe since the 1950s, brought about by the growth of industrial Brazil and the countries of the River Plate region. This dynamic development has produced spectacular sky-scraping cities, expanding industries, and exploitation of mineral and agricultural resources on a hitherto undreamed of scale. The South American countries no longer rely solely on their pastoral and agricultural resources, and acting as markets for imported manufactured goods. These nations themselves now export a considerable range of manufactured and processed goods. Cargo from Brazil these days includes footwear, copper tubes, textiles and other finished products. There is still a large movement of coffee, cotton, cocoa and timber. But there is an increasing tendency for these to be shipped in semi-manufactured or processed form; soluble coffee, cocoa, butter, timber products such as parquet, door lippings, plywoods, and a wide range of veneers and hardwoods. Exports from Argentina include motor vehicle parts and iron and steel products as well as canned meat and fruit, wine as well as wool and animal foodstuffs in bulk, in processed forms such as pellets, extracts and meals. Ships take to Brazil and the River Plate, sophisticated machinery, machine tools, and other equipment for the new factories. Sometimes whole factories or blast furnaces are carried. As part of this industrialisation and development there has been a considerable expansion of their national shipping lines, and these carry a considerable share of the trade.[1]

Lamport and Holt Line, by the mid-1970s had a fine, but nevertheless elderly fleet of four 'R' class vessels. Indications from shippers were that a break bulk vessel with some container capacity would be required in the South American East Coast trades for a number of years to come, and therefore the management set about studying proposals for the best possible replacements for the fleet. The result was to see the ordering in June, 1976 of four of the successful SD14 cargo ships from the yard of Austin and Pickersgill Ltd., Sunderland. The vessels, built to the latest fourth series design, were to be of 15,265 tonnes deadweight and equipped to carry 118-20 ft. containers in the holds, on the hatch covers and on the upper deck. Four of the five holds were fitted with a tween deck whilst the other had provision for the carriage of edible oil. Cargo handling equipment comprising one 26 tonne and three 22 tonne 'Velle' derricks serving the forward hatches and two 5 tonne derricks at No. 5 hatch.

(1) Journal of Commerce—1975.

The four ships were duly completed in 1979 and 1980, and entered service as the 'B' class, named *Bronte* (3), *Browning* (3), *Boswell* (3) and *Belloc*. The older 'R' class vessels being disposed of, the *Romney* (2) and *Roland* (2), being broken up at Faslane in 1978 while the *Ronsard* and *Raeburn* (4) were sold for further trading.

The new vessels joined the Joint British Line's service to the East Coast of South America, comprising Blue Star Line, Houlder Bros., Lamport and Holt Line and Royal Mail Lines, trading as BHLR, where their appearance was most welcome. However their entry into service did regrettably mark the end of the passenger service as, unlike the 'R' class before them, none had any passenger accommodation.

During 1981 the BHLR service was extended to offer a fully containerised sailing from the United Kingdom to the East Coast of South America, using two time-chartered vessels of moderate size, and gradually the demand for container capacity increased. As a result of the Falklands War a larger vessel with greater container capacity was required to transport construction equipment and materials for the new airport, and as a result the four 'B' class ships were gradually disposed of to other owners, and in 1983 the 12,214 gross ton motorship *Ruddbank* was acquired from the Bank Line and renamed *Romney* (3). She saw service outwards to the Falklands and loaded homewards at Montevideo and Brazil, and continued in service until the completion of the project in the South Atlantic. Thereafter she was disposed of.

Meanwhile it was decided to rationalise the BHLR container service by using larger vessels and renaming the service as the Brisa Line (British South America Lines). At the same time the management of the joint service was integrated into one central office at 46/50, Gun Street, London, which marked its incorporation into a consortium of European and South American Lines, operating nine similar container ships within a common schedule. A conventional/break bulk service is also offered from South America to Liverpool, Belfast and Dublin.

As a result of these developments Lamport and Holt Line and Blue Star Line decided to convert an existing group vessel to make her suitable for this service. As a result the *New Zealand Star*, which had been built in 1979 by Smith's Dock Co. Ltd., Middlesbrough, for Blue Star Line's New Zealand—Australia—The Gulf—Karachi—Bombay—Cochin—Colombo—Singapore—New Zealand—service, was selected. She was sent to the Jurong Shipyard at Singapore in January, 1986 for lengthening and refurbishment. This increased her container capacity from 721 to 1,143 and her gross tonnage from 17,082 to 22,635, effectively increasing her capacity by 84 per cent. At the same time her accommodation was refurbished, and facilities for twelve passengers provided in five double and two single cabins with their own private facilities.

On completion of the work, the vessel was repainted in Lamport and Holt Line colours, and renamed *Churchill* after that most respected British Statesman, prolific author and renowned artist. She sailed from Singapore for Montevideo where in April, 1986 she joined the Brisa Line service Northbound. Her schedule takes in the following ports: Tilbury—Hamburg—Bremen—Antwerp—Salvador—Santos—Montevideo—Rio Grande—Sao Francisco do Sul—Santos—Salvador—Rotterdam—Tilbury (with an occasional call at Recife).

On May 12, 1986 the *Churchill* was welcomed at Tilbury Dock where Lady Soames, daughter of the late Sir Winston Churchill, named the vessel, which is the largest ever to carry the company's colours.

The *Churchill* has re-introduced the Lamport and Holt Line passenger service to and from South American East Coast ports and carries on traditions started over 140 years ago by William James Lamport and George Holt.

APPENDICES

APPENDICES

14. APPENDIX ONE
FLEET LIST—SAILING SHIPS

Name and Period in Fleet	Tons	History
Christabel (1) 1845-1846	335	Barque. 1845 built by Charles Lamport, Workington for George Holt, Cotton Broker of Liverpool, 1845 to L + H; 1846 to James Alexander, Workington; 1847 to Harding, London; 1852 to Stranack, London; 1857 condemned.
Junior 1845-1855	677	Barque. 1845 built at Quebec for L + H; 1855 wrecked.
William Ward 1846-1853	755	Ship. 1842 built at St. John for unknown owners; 1846 to L + H; 1853 to Wm. Morgan, Liverpool; No other details.
Julius Caesar 1846-1853	738	Ship. 1838 built at New Brunswick for unknown owners; 1846 to L + H; c1853 omitted.
Emma 1847-1852	—	Ship. 1845 built at Sunderland for George Holt, Cotton Broker of Liverpool; 1847 to L + H; 1852 to Schillizzi, Liverpool; 1860 to J. Smurthwaite, Sunderland; 1863 to G. Seymour, London; 1866 to J. Snowdon. South Shields; c1874 omitted.
Grasmere 1847-1865	454	Ship. 1847 built at Chepstow for L + H; 1865 lost at sea.
Moslem 1848-1853	170	Brig. 1835 built at Yarmouth for J. Vale, London; 1848 to L + H; 1853 to T. Blessett, Liverpool; c1858 omitted.
Thornhill 1848-1855	698	Ship. 1848 built at Quebec for L + H; 1855/56 omittted.
Napan Belle 1849-1856	332	Barque. 1849 built at Nova Scotia for unknown owners, 1849 to L + H; c1856 omitted.

Name and Period in Fleet	Tons	History
Wilhelmina 1849-1852	168	Brig. 1843 built at Maryport for Seymour, Maryport; 1846 to Moss and Company, Liverpool; 1849 to L + H; 1852 to Byers and Company, Workington; 1859/60 abandoned.
Balkan 1849-1863	192	Brigantine. 1849 built at Liverpool for L + H; 1863 to Gambles, Liverpool; c1865 wrecked.
Cathaya 1850-1857	407	Ship. 1850 built by Charles Lamport, Workington, for L + H; 1852 lengthened, tonnage increased to 503; 1857 lost.
Ceres 1850-1855	117	Schooner. 1850 built at Prince Edward Island for L + H; 1855/56 to foreign owners; 1862 to Blaney and Company, Glasgow; c1870 omitted.
Jane Morice 1850-1862	323	Barque. 1850 built at New Brunswick for L + H; 1862 sold; no other details.
Margaret Gibson 1850-1866	124	Brig. 1844 built at Hull for W. Gibson, Hull; 1850 to L + H; 1850 lengthened and tonnage increased to 148; 1866 omitted.
Rydal 1852	262	Barque. 1852 built at New Brunswick for L + H; 1852 to Rathbone Brothers, Liverpool; 1861 to Birleys, Liverpool; 1863/64 lost.
Princeza 1853-1862	149	Brig. 1849 built at Aberdeen for Miller and Company, Liverpool; 1853 to L + H; 1862/63 to unknown owners; 1869/70 wrecked.
Queen 1854-1859	104	Schooner. 1848 built at Teignmouth for A. Owens, Teignmouth; 1854 to L + H; 1859 to Pritchard, Bangor; 1863/64 lost.
Simoda 1855	697	Ship. 1854 built at St. John for unknown owners; 1855 to L + H; c1855 wrecked.
Agenoria 1856-1868	1,023	Ship. 1856 built at New Brunswick for L + H; 1868 to Griffiths and Company, Liverpool; 1868 to Young and Company, North Shields; 1885 broken up at North Shields.

Name and Period in Fleet	Tons	History
Breeze 1855-1868	165	Snow. 1848 built at Annan for J. Nicholson, Annan; 1855 to L + H; 1868 went missing.
Kahlamba 1856-1869	319	Iron Barque. 1856 built by J. Reid and Company, Port Glasgow, for L + H; 1869 to C. de Casas, Rivadeo, renamed *Carlos*; 1884 to John Craig, Greenock, renamed *Kahlamba*; 1885 to Peter Scott, Greenock; 1887 to J. O'Connor, Buenos Aires; 1890 omitted—possibly hulked.
Memphis 1856-1862	416	Barque. 1856 built at St. John for L + H; 1862 to Phillips and Company, Liverpool; 1866 omitted.
Blencathra 1857-1871	466	Barque. 1857 built by Charles Lamport, Workington, for L + H; 1871 sold, no other details.
Coniston 1857-1865	204	Barque. 1857 built by Charles Lamport, Workington, for L + H; 1865/66 wrecked.
Elizabeth Morrow 1857-1860	394	Barque. 1857 built by Cail, New Brunswick, for L + H; 1860 to Walker and Company, Glasgow; 1864 to Cornish and Company, Liverpool; c1870 omitted. (Some doubt regarding L + H ownership).
Glaramara 1857-1863	475	Barque. 1857 built by Charles Lamport, Workington, for L + H; 1863 to Shute and Company, Liverpool; 1865 to Hudson Bay Company, London; 1867 to Brymner and Company, Greenock; 1869/70 burnt out.
Old Harry 1857-1870	156	Ketch. 1843 built at Maidstone for C. Pybus, Rochester; 1857 to L + H; c1870 omitted. (Some doubt regarding L + H ownership).
Rothay 1858-1864	198	Schooner. 1858 built by Charles Lamport, Workington for L + H; 1864 to J. Hainsworth, Liverpool; c1874 omitted.
Thebes 1858-1862	432	Barque. 1850 built at Sunderland for Rathbone and Company, Liverpool; 1858 to L + H; 1862 to E. S. Roberts, London; 1863 to Weinholt and Company, London; c1865 abandoned at sea. (Some doubt regarding L + H ownership).

Name and Period in Fleet	Tons	History
Eddystone 1860-1861	526	Barque. 1860 built at New Brunswick for L + H; 1861 to Young and Son, Shields; 1862 to J. Avery, Shields; c1873 omitted.
Bonnie Dundee 1861-1872	1,027	Ship. 1861 built by McLachlan, New Brunswick for L + H; 1872 to T. Spaight, Limerick; 1879 to H. Ewing. Liverpool; 1882 to H. M. Rummelhoff, Christiania, renamed *Signe*; 1890 omitted.
Chalgrove 1862-1869	509	Barque. 1862 built by Charles Lamport, Workington, for L + H; 1869 to R. Habgood, London; 1878 to Mrs. S. Habgood, London; 1886 to W. Barrett, London; 1889 to Bevan, Evans and Company, London; 1893 to H. J. Larsen, Lillesand; 1896 broken up.
Nazarine 1862-1865	921	Ship. 1854 built at Quebec for Fisher and Sons, Liverpool; 1862 to L + H; 1865 to Curwin and Company, Liverpool; 1869 to W. Geves; 1872 lost.
Christabel (2) 1863-1864	170	Brigantine. 1863 built by Owen, Teignmouth, for L + H; 1864 to H. F. Watt, Liverpool; 1869 to Tonge and Company, Liverpool; 1870 to R. Gladstone, Liverpool; 1876 to Baine and Johnston, Greenock; 1885 to W. B. Grieve, Greenock; l887 to M. Lawrey, Plymouth; l897 to J. Randell, Plymouth; 8.1903 hulked at Plymouth.
Sumroo 1865-1867	612	Barque. 1865 built by Hilyard, New Brunswick, for L + H; 1867 to unknown owners; c1871 omitted.
Timour 1865	1,331	Ship. 1865 built by Hilyard, New Brunswick, for L + H; 1865 to Rathbone Brothers, Liverpool; 1872 to Fernie and Company, Liverpool; 1881 to Alexander Cassels, Liverpool; 1882 to W. H. Ross and Company, Liverpool; c1883 omitted.
March 1866-1867	1,255	Ship. 1866 built by Hilyard, New Brunswick, for L + H; 1867 to Charles Hill and Sons, Bristol, renamed *Glenhaven*; 1872 to W. Rankin, Greenock; 1877 to V. Trayes, Cardiff; 1884 omitted.

Name and Period in Fleet	Tons	History
Manchester 1866-1873	158	Brigantine. 1824 built at Whitehaven for Brocklebank, Whitehaven; 1852 to Armstrong, Workington; 1866 to L + H; 1873 broken up.
Christabel (3) 1867-1869	660	Barque. 1867 built by King, New Brunswick, for L + H; c1869 to Dypois and Burqueue, Nantes, renamed *Formose*; no other details.
Tidal Wave 1867-1868	1,280	Ship. 1867 built by King, New Brunswick, for L + H; 1868 to Fletcher and Parr, Liverpool, renamed *Louisa Fletcher*; 1879 to C. S. Caird, Greenock; 1883 to A. Tischbein and Company, Lussinpiccolo, renamed *Florida*; c1890 to C. H. Evenson, Fredrikstad; no other details.
Sarah J. Eills 1869-1871	1,350	Ship. 1869 built by King, New Brunswick, for L + H; 1871 to W. and R. Wright, Liverpool, renamed *Bride of Corne*; 1878 to Geo. W. Gass, Liverpool; 1886 to Mrs. E. Allen, Liverpool; 1887 stranded; no other details.

15. APPENDIX TWO
FLEET LIST—
STEAMERS AND MOTOR VESSELS

Name and Period in Fleet	Gross Tons	History
Zulu 1857-1858	189	1857 built by Scott and Company, Greenock, for L + H; 1858 to Mauritius owners; 28.5.1861 lost off Jamaica.
Memnon 1861-1883	1,290	1861 built by Scott and Company, Greenock, for L + H; 1883 to Alfred Holt and Company, Liverpool; (Ocean Steamship Company); 1893 to East India Ocean Steamship Company (Alfred Holt and Company), Liverpool; 1899 dismantled to a hulk.
Copernicus (1) 1862-1864	1,372	1862 built by A. Leslie and Company, Hebburn, for L + H; 1864 to Messageries Imperiales, France, renamed *Copernic*; 1871 owners restyled as Messageries Maritimes; 1.1890, sold for breaking up.
Kepler 1863-1903	1,500	1863 built by A. Leslie and Company, Hebburn, for L + H; 1871 lengthened and new engines and boilers fitted, gross tonnage increased to 2,258; 1878 to Belgian flag; 1902 to L + H; 1903 broken up.
Newton (1) 1864-1881	1,329	1864 built by McNab and Company, Greenock, for L + H; 9.4.1881 wrecked off Madeira, on passage Rio de Janeiro to London.
Galileo (1) 1864-1869	—	1864 built by A. Leslie and Company, Hebburn, for L + H; 1869 to T. H. Jackson, Liverpool; renamed *Juan*; 1874 to J. Jack and Company, Liverpool, who re-engined her, completing same in following year; 1878 to J. B. Palmer and Company, London; 1882 to W. Banks, London; 1884 to T. A. Hinton, London; 1888 to Westcott and Lawrence; 1898 to H. Diederichsen, Kiel; 26.8.1898 sailed from Hong Kong for Kiaochow, and went missing.

Name and Period in Fleet	Gross Tons	History
Saladin 1865-1872	510	1856 built by Cato, Miller and Company, Liverpool for Alfred Holt and Company, Liverpool; 1864 to West India and Pacific Steamship Company; 1865 to L + H; 1872 to J. Martin, Liverpool; 1882 omitted.
Talisman 1865-1873	738	1860 built by Scott and Company, Greenock, for Alfred Holt and Company, Liverpool; 1864 to West India and Pacific Steamship Company; 1865 to L + H; 21.1.1873 foundered North West of Burlings, Portugal.
Ptolemy 1865-1896	1,401	1865 built by A. Leslie and Company, Hebburn, for L + H; 1880 new engines fitted; 1896 broken up.
Halley 1865-1895	1,637	1865 built by A. Leslie and Company, Hebburn, for L + H; 1895 broken up by T. W. Ward, Preston.
Herschel (1) 1865-1872	—	1853 built by Laird Brothers, Birkenhead, for the African Steamship Company, Liverpool, but sold while fitting out to Canadian Steamship Company, Liverpool, and completed as *Charity*; 1856 to unknown Spanish owners, renamed *Cubana* or *La Cubana*; 1865 to L + H, renamed *Herschel*; 1872 to R. M. Sloman and Company, Hamburg, and by 1876 at latest had been converted into a sailing ship and renamed *Palmerston*; 1890 to Bruckner and Albers, Hamburg; 1894 to A. Princeti, Genoa, renamed *Frederico;* 1899 condemned and broken up. Some of these details are open to doubt.
Ironsides 1866-1868	691	1865 built by Candlish and Company, Middlesbrough for Girvin and Company, Liverpool; 1866 to L + H; 1868 to D. Jones, Briton Ferry; 1869 to Stowe and Company, Cardiff; 1873/74 omitted.
Cassini 1866-1871	993	1866 built by A. Leslie and Company, Hebburn, for L + H; 1871/72 to R. T. Smyth and Company, Liverpool, (sometimes shown as Paul and Smyth or T. Paul); 1876 to Barrow Shipbuilding Company, Barrow; 1877 to Carruthers and

Name and Period in Fleet	Gross Tons	History
		Johnston, Liverpool; 1879 back to Barrow Shipbuilding Company, Barrow; 1881 to Navigazione Generale Italiana, Genoa; 1.1909 broken up at Palermo.
Copernicus (2) 1866-1883	1,629	1886 built by A. Leslie and Company, Hebburn, for L + H; 1877 to Belgian flag; 2.1883 wrecked at Porto de Pedras, on passage Liverpool to Bahia.
La Plata 1866-1874	1,394	1866 built by A. Leslie and Company, Hebburn, for L + H; 1874 to Bailey and Leatham, Hull; 1875 to unknown owners; 1881 to William Bailey (of Bailey and Leatham); 3.7.1886 wrecked near Thisted, on passage Tyne to Reval.
Donati 1866-1891	1,395	1866 built by A. Leslie and Company, Hebburn, for L + H; 1891 to A. Coote and Company, Liverpool; 10.12.1892 went missing on passage New York to Oporto.
Flamsteed (1) 1866-1873	1,376	1866 built by A. Leslie and Company, Hebburn, for L + H; 24.11.1873 lost in collision with H.M.S. *Bellerophon*.
Laplace (1) 1866-1894	1,410	1866 built by A. Leslie and Company, Hebburn, for L + H; 1874 new engine and boiler fitted; 8.1894 to Comp. Pernambuco de Nav., Brazil, renamed *Capibaribe*; 1917 broken up.
Humboldt 1866-1894	1,638	1866 built by A. Leslie and Company, Hebburn, for L + H; 1880 new engine and boiler fitted; 1894 to Comp. Pernambuco de Nav., Brazil, renamed *Camocim*; 1917 broken up.
Tycho Brahe 1867-1892	1,808	1867 built by A. Leslie and Company, Hebburn, for L + H; 1878 to Belgian flag; 1892 to Charles Wells and Company, London, renamed *Palais Royal*; 1893 to William Hurlbatt, London; 1894 to Idarei Massousieh, Constantinople, renamed *Taif*; 30.10.1908 lost in collision off Sereglio Point at Constantinople, with steamer *Bagdad*.

110

Name and Period in Fleet	Gross Tons	History
Hipparchus 1867-1915	1,863	1867 built by A. Leslie and Company, Hebburn, for L + H; 1878 to Belgian flag; 1895 converted to a hulk; 1.8.1915 sold, no other details.
Pascal (1) 1869-1897	1,950	1869 built by A. Leslie and Company, Hebburn, for L + H; 1878 to Belgian flag; 1887 to L + H; 3.1897 broken up at Genoa.
Olbers 1870-1901	2,162	1870 built by A. Leslie and Company, Hebburn, for L + H; 1882 new engine and boiler fitted; 1886 to Belgian flag; 7.1901 broken up at Genoa.
Biela (1) 1870-1900	2,182	1870 built by A. Leslie and Company, Hebburn, for L + H; 1883 new engine and boiler fitted; 1.10.1900 lost in collision with steamer *Eagle Point* off Nantucket, on passage New York to Liverpool.
Vandyck (1) 1873-1892	1,686	1867 built by Randolph Elder and Company, Fairfield, as *City of Limerick* for Tait and Company, London; 1868/69 to T. and J. Harrison, Liverpool, renamed *Warrior*; 1873 to L + H; 1874 re-engined and renamed *Vandyck*; 1892 converted to a coal hulk at Rio de Janeiro.
Calderon (1) 1871-1887	1,018	1871 built by A. Leslie and Company, Hebburn, for L + H; 1887 to J. N. de Vincenzi, Rio de Janeiro, renamed *Arlindo*; c1890 to Brazilian Coal Company, Rio de Janeiro; c1900 renamed *Caminha*; c1904 to Barcellos and Moura, Rio de Janeiro, renamed *Santa Maria*; believed hulked.
Camoens (1) 1871-1879	1,093	1871 built by A. Leslie and Company, Hebburn, for L + H; 1879 to W. Slimon and Company, Leith; 1888 to Navigazione Generale Italiane, Genoa, renamed *Oreto*; 1914 to Soc. Anon. Vinalcool, Cagliari, renamed *Logudoro*; 1923 broken up in Italy.
Gassendi 1872-1884	1,849	1872 built by Hall, Russell and Company, Aberdeen for L + H; 1885 to T. and J. MacFarlane, Glasgow; 1886 to G. Willison, Liverpool; 1891 to G. B. Reforzo, Genoa, renamed *Madonna Della Costa*; 6.7.1894 lost by fire at Santos.

Name and Period in Fleet	Gross Tons	History
Rubens (1) 1872-1909	1,671	1872 built by Iliff, Mounsey and Company, Sunderland, for L + H; 1909 sold as a hulk at Punta Arenas.
Teniers 1873-1892	1,803	1868 built by R. Elder and Company, Govan, as *City of Rio de Janeiro* for Tait and Company, London; 1870 to W. J. Lamport; 1873 to L + H; 1874 renamed *Teniers*; 1878 to Belgian flag; 4.1892 broken up at Sunderland.
Memling (1) 1873-1885	1,007	1872 built by Gourlay and Company, Dundee, as *Malaga* for Malcolm and Company, London; 1873 to L + H; renamed *Memling*; 1885 to R. Monteith and Company; 1886 to Raeburn and Verel; 21.1.1889 wrecked off Cape Blanco, on passage Saffi to Casablanca.
Lalande (1) 1873-1885	1,048	1873 built by Inglis and Company, Glasgow; for L + H; 1885 to J. Macfarlane, Glasgow; 1886 to Lalande Steamship Co. Ltd. (J. Colquhoun and Company), Glasgow; 1888 to R. D. Purvis and Company, South Shields; 1892 to Marquides Brothers and Macris Brothers, Piraeus, renamed *Phoenix*; c1896 to Merli and Lugaro, Genoa, renamed *Castellaccio;* c1909 to Vassallo and Narizzano, Genoa, renamed *Bersagliere*; 1924 broken up.
Galileo (2) 1873-1899	2,267	1873 built by A. Leslie and Company, Hebburn, for L + H; 1886 to Belgian flag; 1897 to L + H; 8.1899 broken up.
Leibnitz 1873-1896	2,280	1873 built by A. Leslie and Company, Hebburn, for L + H; 1889 to Belgian flag; 1896 broken up.
Maraldi 1873-1875	1,002	1873 built by Whitehaven Shipbuilding Company, Whitehaven, for L + H; 28.2.1875 wrecked near Pernambuco, on passage Montevideo to Antwerp.
Delambre (1) 1873-1896	1,308	1873 built by William Hamilton and Company, Port Glasgow for L + H; 1896 to E. Thirkell and Company, Liverpool; 1897 broken up.

112

Name and Period in Fleet	Gross Tons	History
Thales 1873-1891	1,501	1873 built by Hall, Russell and Company, Aberdeen, for L + H; 1891 to G. Coudert and Fils, France, renamed *Jules Coudert*; 6.1898 broken up at Genoa.
Archimedes (1) 1874-1893	1,561	1874 built by Hall, Russell and Company, Aberdeen, for L + H; 1893 to H. Duchon-Doris and Cie, France, renamed *Helene*; 1900 to G. Louit, Bordeaux; 1902 to Duroto and Beraldo, Italy, renamed *Riconoscenza*; 8.3.1904 wrecked at Montana.
Cervantes (1) 1874-1884	1,131	1874 built by A. Leslie and Company, Hebburn, for L + H; 1884 to Companhia de Nav. Norte-Sul, Rio de Janeiro, renamed *Camillo*; 1895 to J. F. Carvalho Jnr., Rio de Janeiro, renamed *Norte-Sul*; 8.1897 sank in Rio Grande del Norte, on passage Messoro to Santos.
Maskelyne 1874-1903	2,605	1874 built by A. Leslie and Company, Hebburn, for L + H; 1889 to Belgian flag; 31.1.1903 foundered in position 41.35′N, 34.40′W, on passage New Orleans to Antwerp.
Hevelius 1874-1903	2,583	1874 built by A. Leslie and Company, Hebburn, for L + H; 1889 to Belgian flag; 1903 broken up.
Rosse 1875-1898	1,683	1875 built by A. Leslie and Company, Hebburn, for L + H; 1878 to Belgian flag; 1887 to L + H; 1898 to Empreza Ind., Brazil; 1902 to Brazilianische Bank for Deutschland, Hamburg; 1902 broken up at Hamburg.
Canova (1) 1876-1883	1,120	1876 built by A. Leslie and Company, Hebburn, for L + H; 1883 to unknown Brazilian owners, no other details.
Euclid (1) 1877-1898	1,559	1877 built by Hall, Russell and Company, Aberdeen, for L + H; 1898 to Barcellon Mours and Company, Rio de Janeiro; 1903 broken up.

Name and Period in Fleet	Gross Tons	History
Horrox 1877-1903	1,707	1877 built by T. R. Oswald, Southampton, for L + H; 1878 to Belgian flag; 1887 to L + H; 1903 broken up at Naples.
Plato 1877-1892	1,675	1877 built by A. Leslie and Company, Hebburn, for L + H; 1.3.1892 foundered 160 miles off the Scilly Isles, after breaking main shaft on 29.2.1892, on passage Liverpool to Brazil.
Pliny 1878-1882	1,671	1878 built by Barrow Construction Company, Barrow for L + H; 13.5.1882 wrecked off Long Branch, New Jersey, on passage Rio de Janeiro to New York.
Bessel 1878-1895	1,911	1878 built by A. Leslie and Company, Hebburn, for L + H; 22.6.1895 lost in collision with Wilson Line's *Hero* in the English Channel West of the Royal Sovereign Lightship, on passage London to Brazil.
Sirius 1878-1899	2,173	1869 built by A. Leslie and Company, Hebburn, for Star Navigation Co. Ltd. (Rathbone Brothers), Liverpool; 1878 to L + H; 1882 new engine and boiler fitted; 4.1899 broken up at Genoa.
Herschel (2) 1879-1902	1,947	1879 built by A. Leslie and Company, Hebburn, for L + H; 17.11.1901 badly damaged in collision with steamer *Ardeola* in Crosby Channel, Mersey; 1902 broken up by F. Rysdyk, Rotterdam.
Lassell (1) 1879-1900	1,955	1879 built by A. Leslie and Company, Hebburn, for L + H; 1900 to McCaldin Bros., New York; 1917 to D. M. E. Jones, New York; 1920 to Union d'Enterprises Marocaines, Casablanca; 1920 to J. Castanie, Oran, renamed *Sirene*; 1924 broken up in Italy.
Nasmyth (1) 1880-1902	1,991	1880 built by A. Leslie and Company, Hebburn, for L + H; 6.1902 broken up by Cerruti and Sons, Genoa.

114

Name and Period in Fleet	Gross Tons	History
Stella 1880-1894	106	Steam tug;1880 built by Liverpool Forge Company, Liverpool, for L + H; 6.7.1894 sold, no other details.
Mozart 1881-1902	1,994	1881 built by A. Leslie and Company, Hebburn, for L + H; 1902 broken up by F. Rysdyk, Rotterdam.
Strabo (1) 1881-1905	1,959	1881 built by Barrow Construction Company, Barrow, for L + H; 2.1905 broken up at Genoa.
Handel 1881-1902	1,977	1881 built by A. Leslie and Company, Hebburn, for L + H; 1902 to E. Malucci, Ancona, renamed *Guasco*; 1911 broken up at Cadimare.
Cavour (1) 1881-1891	618	1881 built by Scott and Company, Greenock, for L + H; 1891 to Lage Irmaos, Rio de Janeiro, renamed *Itapeva*; c1896 to Cia Nacional de Nav. Costeira, Brazil; 1898 to Brazilian Lighthouse Service, renamed *Commandante Freitas*; 1930 broken up at Rio de Janeiro.
Dalton 1881-1895	2,030	1881 built by A. Leslie and Company, Hebburn, for L + H; 28.9.1895 wrecked on Isle of Islay, on passage New York to Clyde.
Mytilene	1,827	1881 built by Short Bros., Sunderland, for Lumsdon, Byers and Co. Ltd.; Lamport and Holt's records show that they had an interest in this ship, no other details.
Ilios	2,020	1882 built by Short Bros., Sunderland, for Lumsdon, Byers and Co. Ltd.; Lamport and Holt's records show that they had an interest in this ship, no other details.
Holbein (1) 1882-1901	2,050	1882 built by A. Leslie and Company, Hebburn, for L + H; 1901 to Manchester owners; 1901 to Tintore y Cia, Barcelona, renamed *Tambre*; c1907 to Linea de Vapores Tintore; c1916 to Cia Transmediterranea; 1930 broken up.

115

Name and Period in Fleet	Gross Tons	History
Hogarth (1) 1882-1902	2,053	1882 built by A. Leslie and Company, Hebburn, for L + H; 1902 to unknown owners; 1904 to F. Mattarazzo and Company, Santos, renamed *Attilio*; 1922 broken up at Rio de Janeiro.
Flaxman 1882-1903	2,167	1882 built by Oswald, Mordaunt and Company, Southampton, for L + H; 1903 to Empreza de Nav. Salina (Rodrigues Faria and Company), Rio de Janeiro, renamed *Canoe*; 1906 to Cia Comercio de Navegacao, renamed *Jaguaribe*; 1922/23 to Pereira Carneiro and Cia Ltda. (Cia Comercio e Navagacao); 24.8.1932 sank on passage Rio de Janeiro to Manaos.
Chatham (1) 1883-1891	647	1883 built by Scott and Company, Greenock, for L + H; 1891 to Lage Irmaos, Rio de Janeiro, renamed *Itauna*; c1896 to Cia. Nacional de Nav. Costeira; 1931 broken up at Rio de Janeiro.
Canning (1) 1883-1891	645	1883 built by Scott and Company, Greenock, for L + H; 1891 to Lage Irmaos, Rio de Janeiro, renamed *Itatiaya*; c1896 to Cia. Nacional de Nav. Costeira; 1930 broken up at Rio de Janeiro.
Cuvier 1883-1900	2,299	1883 built by A. Leslie and Company, Hebburn, for L + H; 9.3.1900 lost in collision with steamer *Dovre* off the East Goodwin Lightship, on passage Antwerp to Brazil.
Buffon 1883-1908	2,304	1883 built by A. Leslie and Company, Hebburn, for L + H; 1908 to Cia. Comercio de Navagacao, Brazil, renamed *Tijuca*; 20.5.1917 torpedoed and sunk off Ushant.
Amadeo 1884-1892	411	1884 built by Liverpool Forge Company, Liverpool, for A.S.L.; 1.10.1892 to J. Menendez, Punta Arenas; 1909/14 owners restyled as Soc. Anon. Ganadera y Comercial Menendez y Behety, Punta Arenas; 1929 Port of registry changed to Magallenes; 1930s beached in the Straits of Magellan, at San Gregorio; wreck of the ship survives at this location to this day.

Name and Period in Fleet	Gross Tons	History
Brenda 1884-1893	411	1884 built by Liverpool Forge Company, Liverpool, for A.S.L.; c1893 wrecked, no other details.
Caxton 1885-1895	2,687	1883 built by Oswald, Mordaunt and Company, Southampton, as *Test* for T. R. Oswald, Liverpool; 1885 to L + H, renamed *Caxton*; 1895 to T. Hogan and Sons, renamed *Mendota*; 1900 to C. Parodi di A., Genoa, renamed *Angiolina*; 1905 renamed *Citta di New York*; 1907 to A. Parodi fu B., Genoa, renamed *Constanza*; 1911 to G. Palazio, Italy; 14.8.1917 torpedoed and sunk in the North Sea.
Garrick 1885-1906	2,561	1885 built by A. Leslie and Company, Hebburn, for L + H; 1906 to Acties Sandefjord Hvalfangerselskab (P. Bogan), Sandefjord, as a whaling ship, renamed *Fridtjof Nansen*; 10.11.1906 wrecked at South Georgia Island.
Spenser (1) 1885-1895	2,577	1885 built by Oswald, Mordaunt and Company, Southampton, for L + H; 1895 to T. Hogan and Sons, renamed *Manitou*; 1899 to G. B. Sturlese, Genoa, renamed *Ida*; 8.1909 broken up in Italy.
Dryden (1) 1885-1895	2,743	1885 built by A. Leslie and Company, Hebburn, for L + H; 1895 to T. Hogan and Sons, renamed *Menemsha*; 1898 to United States Navy, renamed *Iris*; 1921 to Swayne and Hoyt, U.S.A.; 1928 broken up at San Francisco.
Como 1885-1889	477	1885 built by Barrow Shipbuilding Company, Barrow, for A.S.L.; c1889 wrecked, no other details.
Delta 1886-1888	289	1886 built by J. Jones and Sons, Liverpool, for A.S.L.; 4.1888 to La Platense Flotilla Co. Ltd., Glasgow; 1893 to N. Mihanovich, Buenos Aires; 1904/07 to P. Besana, Buenos Aires; 1917 no other details.
Elena 1886-1888	289	1886 built by J. Jones and Sons, Liverpool, for A.S.L.; 3.1888 to La Platense Flotilla Co. Ltd., Glasgow; 1892 to the Brazilian Government, Rio Grande do Sul; 1904/07 no other details.

117

Name and Period in Fleet	Gross Tons	History
Chaucer (1) 1886-1913	2,769	1886 built by Hawthorn, Leslie and Co. Ltd., Hebburn, for L + H; 1913 broken up by G. Longueville, Dunkirk.
Siddons (1) 1886-1894	2,846	1886 built by Oswald, Mordaunt and Company, Southampton, for L + H; 1894 to Bellingall and Garroway, Glasgow; 18.4.1896 lost in collision with steamer *Craigearb*, off Norderney, on passage Odessa to Hamburg.
Copernicus (3) 1888-1895	3,230	1887 built by Oswald, Mordaunt and Company, Southampton, as *Lilian* for E. Bates and Sons, Liverpool; 1888 to L + H, renamed *Copernicus*; 16.10.1895 went missing on passage from Sandy Point to Valparaiso.
Newton (2) 1888-1910	2,540	1888 built by Hawthorn, Leslie and Co. Ltd., Hebburn, for L + H; 1910 broken up at Antwerp.
Milton 1888-1911	2,679	1888 built by D. and W. Henderson and Co. Ltd., Glasgow, for L + H; 15.6.1911 wrecked off Portugal, near Cabo Espichel, on passage London to Santos.
Freda 1888-1898	498	1888 built by Naval Construction and Armament Co. Ltd., Barrow, for A.S.L.; 7.7.1898 sold, no other details.
Gerda 1888-1898	498	1888 built by Naval Construction and Armament Co. Ltd., Barrow, for A.S.L.; 1898 to J. G. Nogueira, Rio de Janeiro, renamed *Allianca*; 1909/14 to B. A. Antunes and Company, Para; c1917 no other details.
Wordsworth 1889-1902	3,260	1882 built by A. Leslie and Company, Hebburn, as *Capella* for Star Navigation Company (Rathbone Bros.), Liverpool; 1889 to L + H, renamed *Wordsworth*; 1890 to Belgian flag; 1.8.1902 wrecked near Bahia, on passage from New York.

Name and Period in Fleet	Gross Tons	History
Coleridge 1889-1904	2,610	1875 built by A. Leslie and Company, Hebburn, as *Mira* for Star Navigation Company (Rathbone Bros.), Liverpool; 1889 to L + H, renamed *Coleridge*; 1890 to Belgian flag; 1890 new engine and boiler fitted; 1892 to L + H; 6.1904 broken up at Marseilles.
Hilda 1889-1895	537	1889 built by Naval Construction and Armament Co. Ltd., Barrow, for A.S.L.; 1895 no other details.
Ida 1889-1899	561	1889 built by Naval Construction and Armament Co. Ltd., Barrow, for A.S.L.; 3.10.1899 to N. Mihanovich, Buenos Aires; 1907/09 to Soc. Anon. Sud Atlantica, Buenos Aires; 1917 no other details.
Luna 1889-1894	193	1889 built by Cochran and Company, Birkenhead, for L + H; 17.8.1894 to N. Mihanovich, Buenos Aires; 1907 owners restyled as Nav. a Vap. Nicolas Mihanovich Ltda., Buenos Aires; 1913 owners restyled as Cia. Argentina de Nav. Nicolas Mihanovich Ltda., Buenos Aires; 1923 to Cia. Uruguaya de Nav. Ltda, Montevideo; 1924 registry transferred to Buenos Aires, same owners; 1933 converted to motor vessel, gross tonnage increased to 237; 1942 to Cia. de Nav. Dodero (Compania de Navegacion Fluvial Argentina S.A.), Buenos Aires; mid-1960s reported as still in service; 1976 report received, unconfirmed, that vessel is beached and abandoned in the River Plate.
No. 1 Alsina 1889-1949	274	Lighter. 1889 built by W. H. Potter and Son, Liverpool, for L + H; later renamed *Alsina*; 1949 to Anglo Frigrifico, Buenos Aires; 22.12.1953 British registry certificate surrendered, no other details.
No. 2 Balcarce 1889-1930	274	Lighter. 1889 built by W. H. Potter and Son, Liverpool, for L + H; later renamed *Balcarce*; still trading in mid-1930s, no other details.

Name and Period in Fleet	Gross Tons	History
No. 3 1890-1891	274	Lighter. 1890 built by W. H. Potter and Son Liverpool, for L + H; 1891 wrecked, no other details.
Chantrey 1890-1896	2,788	1890 built by Hawthorn, Leslie and Co. Ltd., Hebburn, for L + H; 17.10.1896 wrecked near Valparaiso, on passage from Quayaquil.
Phidias (1) 1890-1911	2,822	1890 built by Hawthorn, Leslie and Co., Ltd., Hebburn, for L + H; 1911 to Cia. Comercio de Navegacao, Brazil, renamed *Tupy*; 21.9.1918 wrecked near Agadir.
Flamsteed (2) 1892-1893	3,381	1892 built by Hawthorn, Leslie and Co. Ltd., Hebburn, for L + H; 26.3.1893 wrecked on coast of Chile, near Imperial River, on passage Antwerp to Valparaiso; wreck sold and broken up as lies.
Homer 1895-1912	2,585	1895 built by Sir Raylton Dixon and Co. Ltd., Middlesbrough, for L + H; 1912 to Urige y Egiraun, Montevideo; 1914 to Spanish flag, same owner in Uruguay, renamed *Odila*; 1915 to Norwegian owners, renamed *Solbakken*; 4.2.1917 torpedoed and sunk off Cape Finisterre.
Horace 1895-1916	3,335	1895 built by D. and W. Henderson and Co. Ltd., Glasgow, for L + H; 9.2.1916 sunk by raider *Moewe*, 600 miles N.E. of Pernambuco.
Canova (2) 1895-1917	4,637	1895 built by D. and W. Henderson and Co. Ltd., Glasgow, for L + H; 1901 to Belgian flag; 1908 to L + H; 24.12.1917 torpedoed and sunk 15 miles South of Mine Head, Ireland.
Cavour (2) 1895-1929	4,978	1895 built by Sir Raylton Dixon and Co. Ltd., Middlesbrough, for L + H; 3.1929 to Holland for scrap; 6.1929 resold and broken up at Danzig.
Cervantes (2) 1895-1914	4,635	1895 built by D. and W. Henderson and Co. Ltd., Glasgow, for L + H; 1902 to Belgian flag; 1908 to L + H; 8.10.1914 lost by enemy action with cruiser *Karlsruhe*, 100 miles S.W. of St. Paul's Rocks.

Name and Period in Fleet	Gross Tons	History
Juanita 1895-1899	719	1895 built by D. and W. Henderson and Co. Ltd., Glasgow, for A.S.L.; 31.10.1899 to N. Mihanovich, Buenos Aires; 1907/09 to Soc. Anon. Sud Atlantica, Buenos Aires; 1917 no other details.
Canning (2) 1896-1921	5,366	1896 built by D. and W. Henderson and Co. Ltd., Glasgow, for L + H; 1914 requisitioned by the Admiralty for service as a balloon ship—H.M.S. *Canning*; 1919 returned to L + H; 1921 to J. Vassiliou, Greece, renamed *Okeanis*; 1924 to Pittaluga, Italy, renamed *Arenzano;* 1925 broken up.
Virgil (1) 1896-1924	3,338	1896 built by D. and W. Henderson and Co. Ltd., Glasgow, for L + H; 3.1924 broken up by Schweitzer and Oppler, Germany.
Sallust (1) 1898-1924	3,628	1898 built by Sir Raylton Dixon and Co. Ltd., Middlesbrough, for L + H; 1924 broken up by M. Ster and Company, Hamburg.
Raphael (1) 1898-1930	5,855	1898 built by D. and W. Henderson and Co. Ltd., Glasgow, for L + H; 1930 broken by T. W. Ward, Morecambe.
Romney (1) 1899-1926	4,501	1899 built by Sir Raylton Dixon and Co. Ltd., Middlesbrough, for L + H; 12.1926 broken up by Petersen and Albeck, Copenhagen.
Rembrandt 1899-1922	4,667	1899 built by D. and W. Henderson and Co. Ltd., Glasgow, for L + H; 3.1922 broken up in Germany.
Raeburn (1) 1900-1931	6,511	1900 built by D. and W. Henderson and Co. Ltd., Glasgow, for L + H; 4.1931 broken up at Savona.
Rossetti (1) 1900-1929	6,540	1900 built by D. and W. Henderson and Co. Ltd., Glasgow, for L + H; 1929 broken up at Danzig.
Camoens (2) 1900-1924	4,070	1900 built by Workman, Clark and Co. Ltd., Belfast, for L + H; 1901 to Belgian flag; 1908 to L + H; 3.1924 to Germany for scrap; 9.1924 resold to A. Arditi, Genoa, and broken up.

Name and Period in Fleet	Gross Tons	History
Calderon (2) 1900-1912	4,083	1900 built by Workman, Clark and Co. Ltd., Belfast, for L + H; 1901 to Belgian flag; 1908 to L + H; 23.1.1912 broke in two after collision with vessel *Musketeer*, in Crosby Channel, River Mersey.
Thespis 1901-1930	4,343	1901 built by Sir Raylton Dixon and Co. Ltd., Middlesbrough, for L + H; 4.1930 broken up by Hughes, Bolckow and Company, Blyth.
Tennyson 1902-1922	3,901	1900 built by A. Stephen and Sons Ltd., Glasgow, as *Evangeline* for Furness, Withy and Co. Ltd.; 1902 to L + H, renamed *Tennyson*; 1922 to Soc. Anon. Comercial Braun and Blanchard, Chile, renamed *Valparaiso*; 1932 broken up in Italy.
Byron (1) 1902-1922	3,909	1901 built by A. Stephen and Sons Ltd., Glasgow, as *Loyalist* for Furness, Withy and Co. Ltd.; 1902 to L + H, renamed *Byron*; 1922 to Soc. Anon. Comercial Braun and Blanchard, Chile, renamed *Santiago*; 1932 broken up in Italy.
Terence 1902-1917	4,309	1902 built by D. and W. Henderson and Co. Ltd., Glasgow, for L + H; 28.4.1917 torpedoed and sunk N.W. of Fastnet.
Titian 1902-1917	4,170	1902 built by Workman, Clark and Co. Ltd., Belfast, for L + H; 26.8.1917 torpedoed and sunk S.E. of Malta.
Tintoretto 1902-1930	4,181	1902 built by Workman, Clark and Co. Ltd., Belfast, for L + H; 3.1930 broken up at Savona.
Inventor 1905-1918	2,291	1878 built by Aitken and Mansel, Glasgow, as *Inventor* for T. and J. Harrison, Liverpool; 1905 to L + H, and converted into a storage hulk; 5.1918 sold, no other details.
Velasquez 1906-1908	7,542	1906 built by Sir Raylton Dixon and Co. Ltd., Middlesbrough, for L + H; 16.10.1908 wrecked at Sao Sebastiano, near Santos, on voyage Buenos Aires to New York.

Name and Period in Fleet	Gross Tons	History
Veronese 1906-1913	7,877	1906 built by Workman, Clark and Co. Ltd., Belfast, for L + H; 16.1.1913 wrecked near Leixoes, on voyage Mersey to River Plate.
Voltaire (1) 1907-1916	8,615	1907 built by D. and W. Henderson and Co. Ltd., Glasgow, for L + H; 2.12.1916 sunk by the raider *Moewe* 650 miles West of Fastnet.
Verdi (1) 1907-1917	7,120	1907 built by Workman, Clark and Co. Ltd., Belfast, for L + H; 22.8.1917 torpedoed and sunk 115 miles N.W. of Eagle Island, Irish Sea.
Colbert 1908-1917	5,393	1908 built by Forges and Chantiers de la Mediteranee, Havre, for E. Groses, Havre, who had 51 per cent of ship, and L + H who had 49 per cent; 30.4.1917 torpedoed and sunk in Mediterranean. (Traded under the French flag.)
Vasari 1909-1928	10,117	1909 built by Sir Raylton Dixon and Co. Ltd., Middlesbrough, for L + H; 1928 to Hellyer Bros., Hull, converted into a Fish Factory Ship, and renamed *Arctic Queen*; 1935 to U.S.S.R., renamed *Pishchevaya Industriya*; 1979 broken up at Kaohsiung.
Kentmere 1909-1924	2,525	4-master iron full rigged ship. 1883 built by W. H. Potter and Sons, Liverpool, for Fisher and Sprott, London; 1896 to G. Croshaw and Company, London; 1897 to F. E. Bliss, London; 1898 to Anglo-American Oil Co. Ltd. (Kentmere Sailing Ship Co. Ltd.), London, (F. E. Bliss, manager); and converted to a 4-masted barque; 1909 to Pacific Steam Navigation Co. Ltd., Liverpool, for £4,500 and hulked at Punta Arenas; 6.9.1909 to L + H; for use as a storage hulk at Punta Arenas; 28.3.1924 sold, no other details.
Siddons (2) 1911-1923	4,186	1910 built by Armstrong, Whitworth and Co. Ltd.; Newcastle, as *Tremont* for E. C. Thin and Co. Ltd.; 1911 to L + H, renamed *Siddons*; 1923 to R. J. Thomas, renamed *Cambrian Maid*; 10.1931 broken up by Hughes, Bolckow and Co. Ltd., Blyth.

Name and Period in Fleet	Gross Tons	History
Vandyck (2) 1911-1914	10,327	1911 built by Workman, Clark and Co. Ltd., Belfast, for L + H; 26.10.1914 sunk by the raider *Karlsruhe*, 690 miles West of St. Paul's Rocks.
Spenser (2) 1912-1918	4,186	1910 built by Armstrong, Whitworth and Co. Ltd., Newcastle, as *Tripoli* for E. C. Thin and Co. Ltd.; 1912 to L + H, renamed *Spenser*; 6.1.1918 torpedoed and sunk off Bardsey Island, Irish Sea.
Vauban 1912-1932	10,660	1912 built by Workman, Clark and Co. Ltd., Belfast, for L + H; 1913 chartered to Royal Mail Steam Packet Co. Ltd., renamed *Alcala*; 1913 charter ended, renamed *Vauban*; 9.1930 laid up at Southampton; 1.1932 broken up by T. W. Ward, Milford Haven.
Vestris 1912-1928	10,494	1912 built by Workman, Clark and Co. Ltd., Belfast, for L + H; 12.11.1928 foundered off Virginia Cape, on passage from New York to South America, via Barbados.
Dryden (2) 1912-1932	5,839	1912 built by Wm. Hamilton and Co. Ltd., Port Glasgow; ordered by Lancashire Shipping Co. Ltd., as *Bolton Castle*, but sold on stocks to L + H and completed as *Dryden*; 1932 to Coumantaros, Greece, renamed *Panagiotis Th. Coumantaros*; 1939 to J. Vassiliou, Greece; 1940 to S. Niarchos, Greece, renamed *Evgenia*; 16.5.1940 sunk by air attack off Ostend.
Archimedes (2) 1912-1932	5,364	1911 built by Russell and Co. Ltd., Port Glasgow, as *Den of Airlie*; for Den of Airlie Co. Ltd. (C. Barrie and Son, managers); 1912 to L + H, renamed *Archimedes*; 1932 to Wm. Thompson and Company, Leith, renamed *Benmacdhui*; 10.2.1941 damaged by air attack off Yarmouth; 21.12.1941 sunk by mine in position 53.40'N, 00.30'E—10 miles E.N.E. of Spurn Head, while on passage from Immingham to Hong Kong.

Former Lamport and Holt liner "Plutarch" of 1913 is being broken up
at Split as the "Durmitor"

employed in the tramp trade, but finally reached the end of her career in September with her arrival at the shipbreaking yard of Brodospas, at Split, where her demolition is now well advanced.

A report from Sydney, N.S.W. brings the news that the Adelaide Steamship Co., Ltd. and McIlwraith McEacharn, Ltd. have agreed to merge their inter-state shipping operations by the formation of a new company, Associated Steamships, Pty., Ltd., which will control 14 vessels. McIlwraith McEacharn will own about 60 per cent of the company, with the Adelaide Steamship Co., Ltd. owning the remainder.

The decision follows more than seven months of negotiation between the two groups. Earlier negotiations had centred round a complete merger of the two companies. In addition to the 14 vessels, 10 from McIlwraith McEacharn and four from the Adelaide Steamship Co., Ltd., the new company will acquire certain ancillary undertakings. These include terminals at Melbourne and Fremantle, shareholdings

Name and Period in Fleet	Gross Tons	History
Euclid (2) 1912-1931	4,770	1911 built by Northumberland Shipbuilding Co. Ltd., Newcastle, as *Horley* for Houlder, Middleton and Co. Ltd., London; 1912 to L + H, renamed *Euclid*; 1931 to Wm. Thompson and Company, Leith; renamed *Benvannoch*; 1936 to Moller Line Ltd., Shanghai, (British flag), renamed *Marie Moller*; 22.3.1937 burnt out off Holyhead, on passage India to Liverpool, and declared a Constructive Total Loss; 1937 broken up by West of Scotland Shipbreaking Co. Ltd., Troon.
Pascal (2) 1913-1916	5,587	1913 built by A. McMillan and Son Ltd., Dumbarton, for L + H; 17.12.1916 torpedoed and sunk off the Casquets.
Phidias (2) 1913-1941	5,623	1913 built by A. McMillan and Son Ltd., Dumbarton, for L + H; 8.6.1941 torpedoed and sunk North of the Azores.
Plutarch 1913-1931	5,613	1913 built by Russell and Co. Ltd., Port Glasgow, for L + H; 1931 to Yugoslavian owners, renamed *Durmitor*; 21.10.1940 captured by the raider *Atlantis* near Sunda Strait; 2.1941 retaken by H.M.S. *Shropshire* at Mogadishu; 1943 placed under British flag—Ministry of War Transport, renamed *Radwinter*; 1946 handed back to Yugoslavian owners, renamed *Durmitor*; 9.1963 arrived at Split for breaking up.
Socrates 1913-1930	4,979	1913 built by Russell and Co. Ltd., Port Glasgow, for L + H; 1930 to D. P. Margaronis, Greece, renamed *P. Margaronis*; 8.3.1940 torpedoed and sunk S.W. of Land's End.
Strabo (2) 1913-1932	4,930	1913 built by A. McMillan and Son Ltd., Dumbarton, for L + H; 1932 to Atlanticos Steamship Co. Ltd. (Kulukundis Bros.), Syria, renamed *Pauline*; 1933 to R. Olivier, Panama; 1934 to Greek flag, renamed *Pavlina*; 1935 to Bright Navigation Co. Ltd., renamed *Brightvega*; 1936 to N. C. Wan, renamed *Shou Sing*; 1938 to Yamashita K. K.,

Name and Period in Fleet	Gross Tons	History
		Japan, renamed *Yamayuri Maru*; 24.1.1944 bombed and sunk by United States Air Force off Bougainville.
Anta 1913	268	Steam tug. 1912 built by Fabriech Delopthaven, Rotterdam, for J. Constant, London, as *Salado II*; 6.1913 to L + H for £1,900 and renamed *Anta*; no other details.
Herschel (3) 1914-1934	6,293	1914 built by D. and W. Henderson and Co. Ltd., Glasgow, for L + H; 1934 broken up in Italy.
Holbein (2) 1915-1935	6,278	1915 built by D. and W. Henderson and Co. Ltd., Glasgow, for L + H; 1935 broken up in Italy.
Memling (2) 1915-1917	7,307	1915 built by A. McMillan and Son Ltd., Dumbarton, for L + H; 3.10.1917 torpedoed and damaged off Brest, declared a Constructive Total Loss, and broken up.
Meissonier 1915-1930	7,206	1915 built by Russell and Co. Ltd., Port Glasgow, for L + H; 1930 to H. and W. Nelson Ltd., London; 1932 to Royal Mail Lines Ltd., 1933 renamed *Nasina*; 1935 to Garibaldi, Italy, renamed *Asmara*; 11.8.1943 torpedoed and sunk by H.M.S. *Unshaken*, off Brindisi.
Murillo (1) 1915-1930	7,206	1915 built by Russell and Co. Ltd., Port Glasgow, for L + H; 1930 to H. and W. Nelson Ltd., London; 1932 to Royal Mail Lines Ltd.; renamed *Nalon*; 6.11.1940 bombed and sunk by aircraft West of Ireland, while homeward bound from Cape Town.
Moliere 1916-1929	7,206	1916 built by Russell and Co. Ltd., Port Glasgow, for L + H; 1929 to H. and W. Nelson Ltd., London; 1932 to Royal Mail Lines Ltd., renamed *Nela*; 1.1946 broken up by Van Heyghen Freres, Ghent.

Name and Period in Fleet	Gross Tons	History
Marconi 1917-1937	7,402	1917 built by Harland and Wolff Ltd., Glasgow, for L + H; 1937 to Kaye, Son and Co. Ltd., London. (Marconi Steamship Co. Ltd.); 21.5.1941 torpedoed and sunk S.E. of Cape Farewell.
Millais (1) 1917-1938	7,224	1917 built by Harland and Wolff Ltd., Glasgow, for L + H; 1938 to Blue Star Line Ltd., London, renamed *Scottish Star*; 20.2.1942 torpedoed and sunk East of Barbados, in position 13.24′N, 49.36′W, on passage Liverpool to Montevideo.
Swinburne 1917-1941	4,659	1917 built by A. McMillan and Son Ltd., Dumbarton, for L + H; 26.2.1941 bombed by aircraft West of Ireland, then torpedoed and sunk.
Sheridan (1) 1917-1947	4,665	1917 built by A. McMillan and Son Ltd., Dumbarton, for L + H; 1947 to Alexandria Navigation Co. Ltd., renamed *Star of Cairo*; 1950 to Transoceanic Steamship Company, Pakistan, renamed *Ocean Endeavour*; 1963 broken up in Pakistan.
Laplace (2) 1919-1942	7,327	1919 built by A. McMillan and Son Ltd., Dumbarton, for L + H; 29.10.1942 torpedoed and sunk S.E. of Cape Agulhas.
Nasmyth (2) 1919-1938	6,509	1919 built by Harland and Wolff Ltd., Belfast, as *War Vision* for the Shipping Controller; 1919 to L + H, renamed *Nasmyth*; 11.1938 broken up by F. Rysdyk, Rotterdam in damaged condition following stranding at Tanife Point, South Grand Canary Island on 1.5.1938.
Newton (3) 1919-1933	6,509	1919 built by Harland and Wolff Ltd., Belfast, as *War Justice* for the Shipping Controller; 1919 to L + H, renamed *Newton*; 1933 to Rethymnis and Kulukundis, Greece, renamed *Mount Othrys*; 6.1.1945 lost in collision in the River Thames, on passage St. John, New Brunswick to London; declared a Constructive Total Loss, and broken up.

Name and Period in Fleet	Gross Tons	History
Biela (2) 1919-1942	5,298	1918 built by Short Bros. Ltd., Sunderland, as *War Mastiff* for the Shipping Controller; 1919 to L + H, renamed *Biela*; 14.2.1942 missing, presumed torpedoed and sunk East of Cape Race, on passage Liverpool to Buenos Aires.
Bernini 1919-1933	5,242	1918 built by W. Dobson and Co. Ltd., Newcastle, as *War Penguin* for the Shipping Controller; 1919 to L + H, renamed *Bernini*; 1933 to Rethymnis and Kulukundis, Greece, renamed *Mount Dirfys*; 26.12.1936 wrecked on Frying Pan Shoals, Norfolk, Va.
Delambre (2) 1919-1940	7,032	1917 built by Mitsubishi Zosen Kaisha, Nagasaki, as *War Dame* for the Shipping Controller; 1919 to L + H, renamed *Delambre*; 7.7.1940 sunk by the raider *Thor* N.W. of Ascension Island.
Bronte (1) 1919-1939	5,314	1919 built by A. McMillan and Son Ltd., Dumbarton, as *War Coney* for the Shipping Controller; 1919 to L + H, renamed *Bronte*; 27.10.1939 torpedoed S.W. of Ireland; 30.10.1939 sunk by escort after having tried to tow her in.
Browning (1) 1919-1942	5,332	1919 built by A. McMillan and Son Ltd., Dumbarton, as *War Marten* for the Shipping Controller; 1919 to L + H, renamed *Browning*; 12.11.1942 torpedoed and sunk off Oran, in position 35.53′N, 00.33′W.
Bruyere 1919-1942	5,335	1919 built by A. McMillan and Son Ltd., Dumbarton, as *War Mole* for the Shipping Controller; 1919 to L + H, renamed *Bruyere*; 23.9.1942 torpedoed and sunk S.W. of Freetown by *U125* in position 04.55′N, 17.16′W, on passage Buenos Aires to the United Kingdom.
Balfe 1919-1950	5,369	1919 built by D. and W. Henderson and Co. Ltd., Glasgow, as *War Lupin* for the Shipping Controller; 1919 to L + H, renamed *Balfe*; 1950 to Ali A. Hoborby (Jas. Norris and Company), Liverpool, renamed *Star of Aden*; 1955 to John

Name and Period in Fleet	Gross Tons	History
		Manners and Co. Ltd., Hong Kong, renamed *Sydney Breeze*; 1955 to World Wide Steamship Co. Ltd., Hong Kong, renamed *Golden Beta*; 1.2.1959 arrived at Osaka for breaking up by Mitsubishi Zosen Kaisha.
Bonheur 1920-1940	5,327	1920 built by Harland and Wolff Ltd., Belfast, for the Shipping Controller; 1920 completed for L + H; 15.10.1940 torpedoed and sunk N.W. of Cape Wrath, in position 57.10′N, 08.36′W, on passage Liverpool to Rosario.
Balzac (1) 1920-1941	5,372	1920 built by D. and W. Henderson and Co. Ltd., Glasgow, as *War Yew* for the Shipping Controller; 1920 completed as *Balzac* for L + H; 22.6.1941 sunk by raider *Atlantis*, N.E. of Para, in position 12S, 29W approx., on voyage Rangoon to Liverpool.
Boswell (1) 1920-1933	5,327	1920 built by Harland and Wolff Ltd., Belfast, for the Shipping Controller; 1920 completed for L + H; 1933 to White Steamship Co. Ltd., renamed *Adderstone*; 1937 to J. Gerrard, Norway, renamed *Germa*; 1950 to Wallem and Company, Panama; 1951 to Daichi K.K., Japan, renamed *Norway Maru*; 1958 re-engined; 1968 broken up at Sakai.
Lalande (2) 1920-1950	7,453	1920 built by D. and W. Henderson and Co. Ltd., Glasgow, for L + H; 1950 to Italian owners, renamed *Cristina Maria G*; 1953 to Panamanian owners, (Rasmar Inc.), renamed *Cristina Maria*; 8.8.1959 arrived at Hamburg for breaking up by W. Ritscher.
Leighton 1921-1946	7,412	1921 built by A. McMillan and Son Ltd., Dumbarton, for L + H; 28.8.1946 to Smith and Houston Ltd., Port Glasgow, intended for breaking up; but on 9.8.1947 scuttled in North Atlantic, 100 miles N.W. of Malin Head, with a cargo of gas bombs.

Name and Period in Fleet	Gross Tons	History
Linnell 1921-1939	7,424	1921 built by A. McMillan and Son Ltd., Dumbarton, for L + H; 1939 stranded at Alexandria, refloated, but badly damaged; 23.8.1939 arrived at Troon for breaking up.
Hogarth (2) 1921-1933	8,109	1921 built by D. and W. Henderson and Co. Ltd., Glasgow, for L + H; 17.8.1933 arrived at Port Glasgow for breaking up Smith and Houston Ltd.
Vandyck (3) 1921-1940	13,233	1921 built by Workman, Clark and Co. Ltd., Belfast, for L + H; 10.1939 converted to armed boarding vessel—H.M.S. *Vandyck*; 10.6.1940 bombed and sunk West of Narvik.
Lassell (2) 1922-1941	7,417	1922 built by A. McMillan and Son Ltd., Dumbarton, for L + H; 30.4.1941 torpedoed and sunk S.W. of Cape Verde Islands.
Voltaire (2) 1923-1941	13,248	1923 built by Workman, Clark and Co. Ltd., Belfast, for L + H; 10.1939 converted to armed merchant cruiser—H.M.S. *Voltaire*; 9.4.1941 sunk by the raider *Thor*.
Delius 1937-1954 1958-1961	6,065	1937 built by Harland and Wolff Ltd., Belfast, for L + H; 1941 remeasured, tonnage increased to 7,783 gross; 1954 to B.S.L., renamed *Portland Star*; 1958 bareboat chartered to L + H, renamed *Delius*; 1961 to Cie. Metallurgique et Miniere, renamed *Kettara VII*; 24.2.1962 arrived at Tokyo for breaking up.
Delane 1938-1954	6,054	1938 built by Harland and Wolff Ltd., Belfast, for L + H; 1941 remeasured, tonnage increased to 7,761 gross; 1954 to B.S.L., renamed *Seattle Star*; 1961 to Cie. Metallurgique et Miniere, renamed *Kettara VI*; 13.10.1961 arrived at Hong Kong for breaking up.
Devis (1) 1938-1943	6,054	1938 built by Harland and Wolff Ltd., Belfast, for L + H; 1941 remeasured, tonnage increased to 7,761 gross; 5.7.1943 torpedoed and sunk off the coast of Sicily.

Second World War, the *Delius* twice suffered damage as the result of enemy air attack ; the first occasion was in April 1940 in Romsdalsfjord when taking part in the Norwegian campaign. In November 1943 she was attacked by torpedo-carrying aircraft in the North Atlantic and received damage, but managed to return safely to port.

After the war, the *Delius* continued operating on the Lamport and Holt River Plate service until 1954, when she was transferred to the Blue Star Line, principal company in the Vestey group, and renamed *Portland Star* for service to the North Pacific coast, a trade which Blue Star had taken over from the Donaldson Line. She spent four years on that run and was then transferred back to Lamport and Holt and reverted to her original name of *Delius*.

Spanish ports with occasional trips to North Africa. She still has her original triple-expansion engine, built by the Wallsend Slipway and Engineering Co. Ltd., Wallsend on Tyne. Up to comparatively recent times there were at least two older tankers—the Russian *Chalimian*, dating from 1886 and the Mexican *San Luciano*, built in 1892, but whether these ships are still trading or even still in existence, is open to doubt.

Sold by the Stanhal Navigation Ltda., Panama to Yugoslav ship-breakers, the motorship *Salamat* (4,105 gross tons), is probably better remembered as the Elder Dempster liner *Macgregor Laird*, completed in July 1930 by D. and W. Henderson and Company, Ltd., Glasgow. She came into the news in 1953 when the Shell organisation bought her and fitted her out as an oil prospecting ship under the name of *Shell Quest*. As the *Macgregor Laird* she was one of Elder Dempster's " Explorer "-class of motorships, which also included the *Alfred Jones*, *Edward Blyden*, *Henry Stanley*, *David Livingstone*, *Mary Kingsley*, *Mary Slessor* and *William Wilberforce*. For many years she was in the company's regular liner trade from the United Kingdom and Continent to West Africa and it seemed rather surprising at the time that an organisation like Shell should buy a ship which was then 23 years old for service as an oil prospecting and research ship. Notwithstanding the fact that they spent a considerable sum of money in fitting her out and installing a wide variety of special apparatus, they retained her for only three years before selling her to her present disposers, who originally registered her at Puerto Limon under the Costa Rican flag. Now at the age of 31 she has gone to her last resting place in a Yugoslav scrapyard.

Another well-known ship which has recently been disposed of is the Lamport and Holt motorship *Delius* (7,783 gross tons). Under the new ownership of the Cie. Miniere et Metallurgique, S.A., of Casablanca and flying the Panamanian flag, she left Hull as the *Kettara VII* on October 28 for Casablanca, where she loaded a cargo of scrap for Japan prior to delivery for breaking up.

The *Delius* was the pioneer ship of the " D "-class which began to make their appearance in the Lamport and Holt fleet in 1937. All came from the yard of Harland and Wolff, Ltd., Belfast and although they were generally similar, there were differences in appearance in the later ships of the class, which eventually numbered seven in all. The design was a complete departure from previous Lamport and Holt ships, or indeed, any other British cargo ships, for they had a stream-lined superstructure, with a broad funnel and bridge combined, with some of the bridge accommodation, including that for the master, in the forepart of the funnel casing. This must have been extraordinarily noisy since the exhaust pipes from the 6-cylinder, double-acting, 2-stroke oil engine were adjacent and however efficient the bulkhead insulation may have been, both noise and vibration constituted a problem.

Originally built as open shelter-deckers, the first three ships, *Delius*, *Delane* and *Devis* entered service on the company's Liverpool, Brazil and River Plate route. Their average speed however was only about 13 knots, which seemed disappointing in view of their exaggerated streamlining giving—in the opinion of some observers—a false impression of speed.

In 1941 the three original ships were converted to closed shelter-deckers with a deadweight capacity of some 10,470 tons. During the

The Lamport and Holt liner " Delius "

Name and Period in Fleet	Gross Tons	History
Defoe (1) 1940-1942	6,245	1940 built by Harland and Wolff Ltd., Belfast, for L + H; 1941 remeasured, tonnage increased; 24.9.1942 abandoned on fire following an explosion on board S.W. of Rockall, and subsequently sank; not due to enemy action.
Debrett 1940-1955 1956-1964	6,244	1940 built by Harland and Wolff Ltd., Belfast, for L + H; 1942 remeasured, tonnage increased to 8,104 gross; 1955 bareboat chartered to B.S.L., renamed *Washington Star*; 1956 charter ended, renamed *Debrett*; 1964 to Embajada Cia. Nav. S.A., renamed *Ambasciata*; 28.12.1964 arrived at Osaka for breaking up.
Devis (2) 1944-1955 1956-1962	8,187	1944 built by Harland and Wolff Ltd., Belfast, for L + H; 1955 bareboat chartered to B.S.L. renamed *Oakland Star*; 1956 charter ended, renamed *Devis*; 4.7.1962 arrived at Spezia for breaking up.
Defoe (2) 1945-1954 1958-1966	8,462	1945 built by Harland and Wolff Ltd., Belfast, for L + H; 1954 to B.S.L., renamed *Geelong Star*; 1958 bareboat chartered to L + H, renamed *Defoe*; 1966 to Astrofeliz Cia. Nav. S.A., renamed *Argolis Star*; 1967 to Argolis Shipping Co. S.A., Greece; 29.10.1969 arrived at Shanghai for breaking up.
Memling (3) 1945-1953 1957-1959	7,017	1943 built by Short Bros. Ltd., Sunderland, as *Empire Bardolph* for Ministry of War Transport (managers—Donaldson Line); 1945 to L + H, renamed *Memling*; 1953 to B.S.L., renamed *Vancouver Star*; 1957 to L + H, renamed *Memling*; 1957 to B.S.L., bareboat chartered to L + H; 23.10.1959 arrived at Flushing for breaking up.
Millais (2) 1945-1952	7,001	1942 built by C. Connell and Co. Ltd., Glasgow, as *Empire Geraint* for Ministry of War Transport (managers—Royal Mail Lines Ltd.); 1945 management transferred to L + H; 1945 to L + H, renamed *Millais*; 1952 to B.S.L., renamed *Oregon Star*; 1954 to Iris Shipping and Trading Corp., Liberia, renamed *Captayannis*; 1962 to Paleocrassas Bros.; 1962 broken up at Hendrik-ido-Ambacht.

Name and Period in Fleet	Gross Tons	History

Dryden (3)
1946-1952
Devis (3)
1963-1969

9,942 — 1944 built by Lithgows Ltd., Port Glasgow, as *Empire Haig* for Ministry of War Transport; (managers—Ellerman Wilson Line); 1946 to L + H, renamed *Dryden*; 1952 to B.S.L., renamed *Fremantle Star*; 1956 renamed *Catalina Star*; 1963 bareboat chartered to L + H, renamed *Devis*; 1966 to L + H; 1969 to Bry Overseas Nav. Inc., renamed *Mondia*; 12.1969 broken up in Taiwan.

Murillo (2)
1946-1952

7,046 — 1942 built by Lithgows Ltd., Port Glasgow, as *Empire Galahad* for Ministry of War Transport (managers—B.S.L.); 1946 to B.S.L., renamed *Celtic Star*; 1946 to L + H, renamed *Murillo*; 1952 to Industriale Maritime S.p.A., Genoa, renamed *Bogliasco*; 1963 to Ocean Shipping and Enterprises S.A., Panama, renamed *Ocean Peace*; 13.9.1967 arrived at Kaohsuing for breaking up.

George Salt
1946

77 — Steam tug. 1936 built by Henry Robb Ltd., Leith, as *George Salt* for Blackfriars Lighterage and Cartage Co. Ltd. (managers—B.S.L.) London; 1936 to Frederick Leyland and Co. Ltd. (managers—B.S.L.), London; 1946 to L + H; 1946 to Cia. Nav. das Lagaos, Rio Grande do Sul; 1948 renamed *Sao Cristovao*; 1970 still in service, no other details.

Sheridan (2)
1947-1960

3,827 — 1945 built by Consolidated Steel Corp., Wilmington, California, as *Hickory Glen* for United States Maritime Commission, and bareboat chartered to Ministry of War Transport (managers—China Nav. Co. Ltd.); 1947 returned to United States Maritime Commission; 1947 to L + H, renamed *Sheridan*; 1960 to Austasia Line Ltd., Singapore, renamed *Matupi*; 1964 to Kie Hock Shipping (Hong Kong) Co. Ltd., Hong Kong, renamed *Tong Lam*; 1968 to Asia Selatan Enterprises Ltd.; 1970 to Sakota Ltda. S.A., Panama; 27.10.1970 aground in position 15.12'N, 117.44'E, broke in three and became a total loss, on passage from North Korea to Chittagong with a cargo of pig iron.

Name and Period in Fleet	Gross Tons	History
Lassell (3) 1947-1962	7,256	1943 built by Bethlehem Fairfield Shipyard Inc., Baltimore, Md., as *John J. McGraw* for United States Maritime Commission; 1943 bareboat chartered to Ministry of War Transport (managers—L + H); renamed *Samariz*; 1944 renamed *John J. McGraw*; 1947 to L + H, renamed *Lassell*; 1962 to Poseidon Cia. Nav. S.A., Beirut, renamed *Alolos II*; 1967 to Falcon Shipping Company, Cyprus; 1968 broken up at Shanghai.
Byron (2) 1947-1953 *Lalande* (4) 1953-1961	6,902	1940 built by Barclay, Curle and Co. Ltd., Glasgow, as *Empire Voice* for Ministry of War Transport; 1946 to Booth, renamed *Bernard*; 1947 to L + H, renamed *Byron*; 1953 renamed *Lalande*; 1961 to Wm. Brandt, Sons and Company, renamed *Uncle Bart*; 8.9.1961 arrived at Moji for breaking up.
Bronte (2) 1948-1950	4,949	1930 built by Cammell Laird and Co. Ltd., Birkenhead, as *Benedict* for Booth; 1948 to L + H, renamed *Bronte*; 1950 to Turkish owners, renamed *Muzaffer*; 1957 resold, renamed *Umran*; 14.2.1961 arrived at Vigo for breaking up.
Vianna 1947-1949		1945 built by Bethlehem Fairfield Shipyard Inc., Baltimore, Md., as *Atlantic City Victory* for United States Maritime Commission; 1947 to Panama Shipping Corp., renamed *Vianna* and bareboat chartered to L + H; 1949 to Cie. Royal Belge Argentina S.A., renamed *Flandres*; 1962 resold, renamed *Taipei Victory*; subsequently broken up.
Villar 1947-1949		1945 built by Permanente Metals Corp., Richmond, California, as *El Reno Victory* for United States Maritime Commission; 1947 to Panama Shipping Corp., renamed *Villar* and bareboat chartered to L + H; 1949 to K.N.S.M., Holland, renamed *Bennekom*; 1966 resold, renamed *Ithaca Victory*; 1968 resold, renamed *Venus Victory*; 4.1970 broken up at Kaohsiung.

133

Name and Period in Fleet	Gross Tons	History
Browning (2) 1949-1951	4,862	1928 built by Hawthorn, Leslie and Co. Ltd., Hebburn, as *Boniface* for Booth; 1949 to L + H, renamed *Browning*; 1951 to Cia. de Nav. Niques, Panama, renamed *Sannicola*; 1951 to Muko Kisen K.K., Japan, renamed *Mizuho Maru*; 28.2.1961 arrived at Mukaishima for breaking up.
Spenser (3) 1950-1955 *Roscoe* 1955-1962	6,334	1935 built by Bremer Vulkan, Vegesack, as *Dusseldorf* for Norddeutseuer Lloyd, Germany; 25.12.1939 captured off the Chilean Coast by H.M.S., *Despatch*; 1940 placed under the Ministry of War Transport, renamed *Poland*; 1940 renamed *Empire Confidence*; 1946 to Alexandria Steam Navigation Co. Ltd.; renamed *Star of El Nil*; 1949 to Ministry of War Transport; 1950 to L + H, renamed *Spenser*; 1955 renamed *Roscoe*; 1962 broken up at Bilbao.
Lalande (3) 1951 ·	7,219	1944 built by Bethlehem Fairfield Shipyard Inc., Baltimore, Md., as *Samnid* for United States Maritime Commission, and bareboat chartered to Ministry of War Transport (managers—B.S.L.); 1946 to B.S.L., renamed *Pacific Star*; 1951 to L + H, renamed *Lalande*; 1951 to Soc. Anon. Importazione Carbon e Nav., Italy, renamed *Ninfea*; 1959 to China Ocean Shipping Company, Shanghai, renamed *Nan Hai 147*; c1979 renamed *Hong QI 147*, believed still in service.
Sallust (2) 1951-1958	2,993	1948 built by Wm. Pickersgill and Sons Ltd., Sunderland, as *Dunstan* for Booth; 1951 to L + H, renamed *Sallust*; 1958 to Booth, renamed *Dunstan*; 1966 renamed *Basil*; 1968 to Cia. Mtma. Viahoulis S.A., Panama, renamed *Christina*; 1969 broken up at Barranquilla, in damaged condition after a fire at Galveston on 3.1.1969.
Laplace (3) 1952-1953	7,283	1944 built by New England Shipbuilding Corp., Portland, Maine, as *Samannan* for United States Maritime Commission, bareboat chartered to Ministry of War Transport (managers—B.S.L.); 1946 to B.S.L.; 1947 renamed *Oregon Star*; 1952

Name and Period in Fleet	Gross Tons	History
		to L + H, renamed *Laplace*; 1953 to San Panteleimon Cia. Nav. S.A., Panama, renamed *San Panteleimon*; 20.4.1967 arrived at Yokosuka for breaking up.
Siddons (3) 1952-1955 *Rubens* (2) 1955-1965 *Rossini* 1967-1970	4,459	1952 built by Wm. Pickersgill and Sons Ltd., Sunderland, as *Siddons* for L + H; 1955 renamed *Rubens*; 1965 bareboat chartered to Booth, renamed *Bernard*; 1967 charter ended, renamed *Rossini*; 1970 to Booth, renamed *Bernard*; 1973 to Sopac Bulk Carriers Co. Inc., Panama, renamed *Berwell Adventure*; 1974 to Booth; 1974 to Overseas Marine Corp., Panama; 1974 to Kelsey Bay Shipping Co. Ltd., Panama, renamed *Al Turab*; 1978 broken up at Gadani Beach.
Romney (2) 1952-1978	8,237	1952 built by Cammell Laird and Co. Ltd., Birkenhead, for L + H; 3.10.1978 arrived at Faslane for breaking up by Shipbreaking Industries Ltd.
Raeburn (2) 1952-1958 *Roland* (2) 1977-1978	8,311	1952 built by Harland and Wolff Ltd., Belfast, as *Raeburn* for L + H; 1958 bareboat chartered to B.S.L., renamed *Colorado Star*; 1972 bareboat chartered to Austasia Line Ltd., Singapore, renamed *Mahsuri*; 1977 charter ended, renamed *Roland*; 5.10.1978 arrived at Faslane for breaking up by Shipbreaking Industries Ltd.
Raphael (2) 1953-1976	7,971	1953 built by Bartram and Sons Ltd., Sunderland, for L + H; 1976 to Carnation Shipping Co. Ltd., Limassol, renamed *Pola Rika*; 1977 to Allegro Marine Co. Ltd., Limassol; 1979 broken up at Gijon.
Dryden (4) 1953-1955 1963-1968	8,293	1939 built by Burmeister and Wain, Copenhagen, as *Columbia Star* for B.S.L., 1950 to L + H, bareboat chartered to B.S.L.; 1953 charter ended, renamed *Dryden*; 1955 bareboat chartered to B.S.L., renamed *Patagonia Star*; 1957 renamed *Columbia Star*; 1959 to B.S.L.; 1963 bareboat chartered to L + H, renamed *Dryden*; 1966 to L + H; 10.11.1968 arrived at Kaohsiung for breaking up.

Name and Period in Fleet	Gross Tons	History

Sargent
1954-1962

3,843

1945 built by Walter Butler Shipbuilders Inc., Duluth, Minn., as *Frank J. Petrarca* for United States Maritime Commission; 1945 renamed *Roband Hitch*; 1946 to Panama Shipping Corp., bareboat chartered to Booth, renamed *Jutahay*; 1954 to L + H, registered at Port of Spain, Trinidad, renamed *Sargent*; 1962 to A. Halcoussis, Greece, renamed *Pamit*; 1966 to Bambero Cia. Nav. S.A., Liberia, renamed *Bambero*; 3.3.1970 arrived at Castellon for breaking up by I. M. Varela Davalillo.

Balzac (2)
1954-1959
Carroll
1959-1960

3,022

1939 built by Burmeister and Wain, Copenhagen, as *Mosdale* for A/S Mosvold Shipping, Norway; 1954 to B.S.L. (originally proposed to rename vessel as *Trinidad Star*, but not carried out), renamed *Albion Star*; 1954 to L + H, renamed *Balzac;* 1959 renamed *Carroll*; 1960 to B.S.L., renamed *Norman Star*; 1960 bareboat chartered to Booth, renamed *Basil*; 1964 to H. and D. Kyriakos, Greece, renamed *Eleni K*; 1966 to Helen Shipping Corporation (Panama) Ltd., Greece, renamed *Eleni Kyriakou*; 1970 renamed *Olga*; 1970 to Kreta Shipping Co. S.A., Greece, renamed *Georgios Markakis*; 1973 to Amarinthos Shipping Co. Ltd., Cyprus, renamed *Nikos S*; 4.5.1973 arrived at Bilbao for breaking up.

Verdi (2)
1955-1963

571

1954 built by N.V. Scheepsbouwwerf v/h De Groot and Van Vliet, Slikkerveer, as *Hermes* for Brinkman, Kunst and Schokkenbroek, Holland; 1955 to L + H, renamed *Verdi*; 1963 to N.V. Scheeps-Exploitatie Maats "Het Gein", Holland, renamed *Kilo*; 1974 to C. Englesos, Cyprus, renamed *Annet*; 1974 transferred to Greek flag, renamed *Katopodis G*; 1977 to Katopodis Bros., Greece; 18.12.1977 stranded in Derna Harbour during voyage from Viareggio.

Boswell (2)
1955-1960
Crome
1960

3,111

1938 built by Burmeister and Wain, Copenhagen, as *Barfleur* for Cie. Generale d'Armament Maritime, France; 1955 to B.S.L.; 1955 to L + H, renamed *Boswell*; 1960 renamed *Crome*; 1960 to B.S.L., renamed *Roman Star*; 1961 bareboat chartered to Booth, renamed *Bede*; 1963 to Rahcassi Shipping Co. S.A., Greece, renamed *Victoria Elena*; 16.1.1967 caught fire while loading a cargo of cotton at Thessalonika, Greece; 19.1.1967 beached in a heavily damaged condition off Piraeus, declared a Constructive Total Loss, refloated; 1967 broken up at La Spezia by Lotti S.p.A.

Virgil (2) 1956-1963	404	1956 built by Schiffsw A. Pahl, Hamburg, launched as *Manstead*; 1956 to Panama Shipping Corp., bareboat chartered to L + H, and renamed *Virgil*; 1963 to N.V. Scheeps—Exploitatie Maats "Het Gein", Holland, renamed *Metre*; 1974 to Ahmed Sayed Issa, Lebanon, renamed *Amina*; 1977 to Hani Ahmed Majzoub and Shikri Khoury and Company, Lebanon; still in service.
Rossetti (2) 1956-1963 1967-1970	4,693	1956 built by Wm. Pickersgill and Sons Ltd., Sunderland, for L + H; 1963 bareboat chartered to Booth, renamed *Boniface*; 1967 charter ended, renamed *Rossetti*; 1970 to Booth, renamed *Boniface*; 1974 to Hydra Navigation Co. Ltd., Greece, renamed *Amaryllis*; 1978 to Imerama S.A., Greece, renamed *Zefyros*; 1979 broken up at Kaohsiung.
Ronsard 1957-1980	7,840	1957 built by Bartram and Sons Ltd., Sunderland, for Salient Shipping Co. (Bermuda) Ltd., Hamilton, and bareboat chartered to L + H; 1960 to L + H; 1980 to Obestain Inc., Panama; renamed *Obestain*; 1981 broken up in Taiwan.
Murillo (3) 1957-1961	7,197	1944 built by Lithgows Ltd., Port Glasgow, as *Empire Talisman* for Ministry of War Transport (managers—B.S.L.); 1946 bareboat chartered to B.S.L., renamed *Tacoma Star*; 1957 to L + H, renamed *Murillo*; 1957 to B.S.L., and bareboat chartered to L + H; 16.3.1961 arrived at Vigo for breaking up.

Name and Period in Fleet	Gross Tons	History

Millais (3)
1957-1960

7,053

1944 built by Short Bros. Ltd., Sunderland, as *Empire Pendennis* for Ministry of War Transport (managers—Ellerman Lines); 1946 to Cunard White Star Ltd., Liverpool, renamed *Vasconia*; 1949 owners restyled as Cunard Steam Ship Co. Ltd.; 1951 to B.S.L., renamed *Fresno Star*; 1957 to L + H, renamed *Millais*; 1957 to B.S.L., and bareboat chartered to L + H; 1960 to Grosvenor Shipping Co. Ltd. (Mollers' Ltd), Hong Kong, renamed *Grosvenor Navigator*; 9.9.1966 arrived at Kaohsiung for breaking up.

Sallust (3)
1958-1959

3,831

1945 built by Leatham D. Smith Shipbuilding Corp., Sturgeon Bay, Wisconsin, for United States Maritime Commission, launched as *Tulare*, completed as *Coastal Challenger*; 1946 to Panama Shipping Corp. bareboat chartered to Booth, renamed *Pachitea*; 1954 to Booth, renamed *Dunstan*; 1958 to L + H, renamed *Sallust*; 1959 to Austasia Line Ltd., Singapore, renamed *Malacca*; 1962 to Kie Hock Shipping (Hong Kong) Ltd., Hong Kong, renamed *Tong Hong*; 25.10.1967 left Kawasaki for Singapore on a voyage to Colombo with a cargo of ammonium sulphate and disappeared; 38 crew lost.

Siddons (4)
1959-1962

1,282

1959 built by Geo. Brown Ltd., Greenock, for L + H, (originally laid down for B.S.L.); 1962 bareboat chartered to Booth, renamed *Veras*; 1966 lengthened at Hamburg, tonnage increased to 1,616; 1973 to Ghania Cia. Nav. S.A., Panama, renamed *Kydonia*; 1976 to Fayrouz Cia. Nav. S.A., Panama, renamed *Fayrouz*; 4.10.1978 damaged by fire at Piraeus, repaired and still in service.

Spenser (4)
1959-1961

1,312

1959 built by Norderwerft Koser and Meyer, Hamburg, for L + H; 1961 to Panama Shipping Corp., bareboat chartered to Booth, and renamed *Valiente*; 1964 lengthened, tonnage increased to 1,609; 1969 renamed *Veloz*; 1973 to Compania National de Nav. S.A., (Navenal), Bogota, renamed *Tanambi*; 23.8.1979 grounded in Panama Canal,

138

Name and Period in Fleet	Gross Tons	History
		while on passage Buena Ventura to Guanta; subsequently refloated; 2.12.1982 arrived at Cartagena, Colombia, for breaking up.
Constable 1959-1962	3,099	1959 built by Brooke Marine Ltd., Lowestoft, for L + H; 1962 to B.S.L., renamed *Santos Star*; 1964 lengthened by Harland and Wolff Ltd., Belfast, tonnage increased to 3,775; 1966 to Calmedia S.p.A. di Nav., Italy, renamed *Calagaribaldi*; 1981 to Nourfo Compania Naviera S.A., Panama, renamed *Gafredo*; 29.4.1984 arrived at Barcelona for breaking up.
Chatham (2) 1960-1962	3,005	1960 built by A. Stephen and Sons Ltd., Linthouse, for L + H; 1962 to B.S.L., renamed *Mendoza Star*; 1963 lengthened at Hoboken, Belgium, tonnage increased to 3,666; 1967 to Calmedia S.p.A. di Nav., Italy, renamed *Calavittoria*; 1979 to Laguna Shipping Co. (Laskaridis Shipping Co. Ltd.), Greece, renamed *Frio Aegean*; 1981 to Tobermory Shipping Co. S.A. (Laskaridis Shipping Co. Ltd), Panama; 26.3.1984 arrived at Gadani Beach for breaking up.
Sheridan (3) 1961-1967	1,535	1961 built by T. van Duijvendijk Scheepswerf N.V. Lekkerkerk, for Booth, bareboat chartered to L + H; 1964 to L + H; 1964 lengthened by Smith's Dock Co. Ltd., North Shields, tonnage increased to 1,849; 1967 bareboat chartered to Booth, renamed *Cyril*; 1973 to Panama Shipping Corp., bareboat chartered to Booth; 1978 to Altis Shipping Co. S.A., Greece, renamed *Angie*; 1979 to Ocean Breeze Cia. Nav. S.A., Greece; 1980 to Aegaeus Maritime Co. S.A., Greece, renamed *Amalia*; 1981 to Wes Line Co. Ltd., Panama, renamed *West Point*; 1985 to Perkapalan Sri Tomah Sendirian Berhad, Malaysia, renamed *Tumoh Saty;* still in service.
Spenser (5) 1962-1967	1,549	1962 built by T. van Duijvendijk Scheepswerf N.V. Lekkerkerk, for Booth, bareboat chartered to L + H; 1964 lengthened at Smith's Dock Co. Ltd.,

Name and Period in Fleet	Gross Tons	History
		North Shields, tonnage increased to 1,869; 1964 to L + H; 1967 bareboat chartered to Booth, renamed *Cuthbert*; 1973 to Panama Shipping Corp., bareboat chartered to Booth; 1977 to Associated Levant Lines S.A.L., Lebanon, renamed *Barouk*; 1982 to Naviera An Hing S. de R.L., Vanuatu, renamed *An Hing*; still in service.
Rossetti (3) 1963-1964		1963 Watts, Watts vessel *Woodford* time chartered to L + H and renamed *Rossetti*; 1964 charter ended, renamed *Woodford*.
Raeburn (3) 1963-1964		1963 Watts, Watts vessel *Wanstead* time chartered to L + H and renamed *Raeburn*; 1964 charter ended, renamed *Wanstead*.
Rossetti (4) 1964		1964 Watts, Watts vessel *Weybridge* time chartered to L + H and renamed *Rossetti*; 1964 charter ended, renamed *Weybridge*.
Rubens (3) 1966-1973	4,472	1951 built by Wm. Pickersgill and Sons Ltd., Sunderland, as *Crispin* for Booth; 1953 to Austasia Line Ltd., Singapore, renamed *Mandowi*; 1966 to Booth, renamed *Dunstan*; 1966 bareboat chartered to L + H, renamed *Rubens*; 1973 to George Kalogeras, Greece, renamed *Irini K*; 24.4.1974 arrived at Istanbul for breaking up.
Renoir 1967-1971	4,300	1953 built by Wm. Pickersgill and Sons Ltd., Sunderland; laid down as *Clement* for Booth, launched as *Malay Star* for B.S.L., and completed as *Malay* for Austasia Line Ltd., Singapore; 1964 renamed *Mahruri*; 1966 to Booth, renamed *Benedict*; 1967 bareboat chartered to L + H, renamed *Renoir*; 1971 to Starlight Steamship Co. S.A., Panama, renamed *Diamond Star*; 1973 broken up at Suao, Taiwan.
Roland (1) 1968-1975	7,344	1950 built by A. Stephen and Sons Ltd., Linthouse; laid down as *Bolton Castle* for Lancashire Shipping Co. Ltd. (Moller's Trust Ltd.), Hong Kong; to B.S.L., whilst on the stocks and completed as the

140

Name and Period in Fleet	Gross Tons	History
		Dunedin Star; 1968 to L + H, renamed *Roland*; 1975 to Pallas Maritime Co. Ltd., Cyprus, renamed *Jessica*; 1975 to Alligator Shipping Co. Ltd., Cyprus; 10.6.1978 arrived at Gadani Beach for breaking up.
Raeburn (4) 1972-1979	6,274	1957 built by Caledon Shipbuilding and Engineering Co. Ltd., Dundee, as *Canadian Star* for B.S.L.; 1972 bareboat chartered to L + H, renamed *Raeburn*; 1975 to L + H; 1979 to Vertigo Shipping Co. Ltd., Panama, renamed *Braeburn*; 1979 to Ahmed Shipping Lines, Panama; 20.4.1979 arrived at Kaohsiung for breaking up.
Bronte (3) 1979-1983	9,324	1979 built by Austin and Pickersgill Ltd., Sunderland, for L + H; 1983 to China Ocean Shipping Company, renamed *An Dong Jiang*; still in service.
Browning (3) 1979-1983	9,324	1979 built by Austin and Pickersgill Ltd., Sunderland, for L + H; 1983 to China Ocean Shipping Company, renamed *An Fu Jiang*; still in service.
Boswell (3) 1979-1983	9,324	1979 built by Austin and Pickersgill Ltd., Sunderland, for L + H; 1983 to Chinese-Tanzanian Joint Shipping Company, China, renamed *Shun Yi*; still in service.
Belloc 1980-1981	9,324	1980 built by Austin and Pickersgill Ltd., Sunderland, for L + H; 1981 to Montenegro Overseas Nav. Ltd. Inc., Panama (Prekookeanske Plovidba, Bar), renamed *Piva*; 1986 Prekookeanske Plovidba, Bar, Yugoslavia; still in service.
Romney (3) 1983-1986	12,214	1979 built by Sunderland Shipbuilders Ltd., Sunderland, as *Ruddbank* for the Bank Line Ltd. (Andrew Weir and Co. Ltd.), London; 1983 to L + H, renamed *Romney*, 1986 sold. Still in service.

Name and Period in Fleet	Gross Tons	History
Churchill 1986-	22,635	1979 built by Smith's Dock Co. Ltd., Middlesbrough, as *New Zealand Star* for Airlease International and New Zealand Star Ltd.; 1983 to New Zealand Star Ltd.; 1986 to L + H, renamed *Churchill*, lengthened, gross tonnage increased from 17,082 to 22,635; present fleet.

ABBREVIATIONS

L + H	=	1. Lamport & Holt (1845-1865).
		2. Liverpool, Brazil and River Plate Steam Navigation Co. Ltd. (Lamport & Holt, Managers) (1865-1911).
		3. Liverpool, Brazil and River Plate Steam Navigation Co. Ltd. (Lamport & Holt Ltd., Managers) (1911-1934).
		4. Lamport & Holt Line Ltd. (1934 to date).
A.S.L.	=	Argentine Steam Lighter Co. Ltd. (Lamport & Holt, Managers)
BELGIAN FLAG	=	Soc. de Nav. Royale Belge Sud-Americaine, Antwerp.
BOOTH	=	Booth Steamship Co. Ltd.
B.S.L.	=	Blue Star Line Ltd.